COMBAT AIRCRAFT

133 **VICKERS WELLINGTON UNITS OF BOMBER COMMAND**

SERIES EDITOR TONY HOLMES

133

COMBAT AIRCRAFT

Michael Napier

VICKERS WELLINGTON UNITS OF BOMBER COMMAND

OSPREY
PUBLISHING

OSPREY PUBLISHING

Bloomsbury Publishing Plc

PO Box 883, Oxford, OX1 9PL, UK

1385 Broadway, 5th Floor, New York, NY 10018, USA

E-mail: info@ospreypublishing.com

www.ospreypublishing.com

OSPREY is a trademark of Osprey Publishing Ltd

First published in Great Britain in 2020

A catalogue record for this book is available from the British Library.

ISBN: PB 9781472840752; eBook 9781472840769; ePDF 9781472840738; XML 9781472840745

20 21 22 23 24 10 9 8 7 6 5 4 3 2 1

Edited by Tony Holmes
Cover Artwork by Mark Postlethwaite
Aircraft Profiles by Janusz Światłoń
Index by Alan Rutter
Originated by PDQ Digital Media Solutions, UK
Printed and bound in India by Replika Press Private Ltd

Osprey Publishing supports the Woodland Trust, the UK's leading woodland conservation charity.

To find out more about our authors and books visit **www.ospreypublishing.com**. Here you will find extracts, author interviews, details of forthcoming events and the option to sign up for our newsletter.

Front Cover

On 18 December 1939 a formation of 22 Wellingtons from Nos 9, 37 and 149 Sqns set out on an unescorted daylight mission to attack German warships in the Schillig Roads and Wilhelmshaven. Intercepted off the German coast by Bf 109s from JG 77 and Bf 110s from II./ZG 76, ten of the bombers were shot down in a running battle. A further two later ditched in the sea and three more landed safely but were damaged beyond repair. This specially commissioned painting by Mark Postlethwaite depicts Wellington IA N2873, which was flown by Sgt F C Petts of No 9 Sqn, under attack from a Bf 110. Petts' aircraft was one of only two Wellingtons to survive from the third section of six bombers, the badly damaged aircraft landing at Sutton Bridge. The engagement, which became known as the Battle of Heligoland Bight, was the trigger for Bomber Command to switch to night operations

Previous Spread

A 4000-lb 'Cookie' bomb is prepared for loading into an unidentified Wellington III. The Wellington was the only aircraft in Bomber Command capable of carrying this high-capacity weapon when it was introduced into frontline service in the early spring of 1941 *(Philip Jarrett)*

ACKNOWLEDGEMENTS

I am deeply indebted to my good friend and colleague Julian Bourn for arranging access to the archives and photographic collection at the Brooklands Museum, and also to Edward Tyack for giving me access to the archives at the Wellington Aviation Museum at Moreton-in-Marsh. I am extremely grateful to Adam Mimpress for hosting me at No 99 Sqn and allowing me free rein over the unit's Wellington material. Thank you, too, to Andrew Thomas and Graham Pitchfork who generously helped with photographs and other research advice, and also to Philip Jarrett for his kindness in providing many of the photographs in this book. Finally, many thanks to Andrew Dennis at the RAF Museum for his assistance with my research.

CONTENTS

INTRODUCTION

The Vickers Wellington has a unique place in the history of the Royal Air Force (RAF), as it was the only bomber to see frontline service from the first day of World War 2 all the way through to the last day of the conflict. At the start of hostilities, it was just one of a number of types operated by Bomber Command, but it soon became the most numerous frontline aircraft in the inventory. Indeed, the Wellington was the mainstay of the RAF bomber offensive against Germany in 1941–42.

Although it was retired from frontline operations by Bomber Command in the autumn of 1943, the Wellington had by then become one of the most important types in service with Coastal Command. Equipped with air-to-surface vessel radar, the Leigh Light and depth-charge bombs, it was heavily involved in the campaign against U-boats in the Atlantic – a role which it performed through to VE-Day. Meanwhile, the Wellington remained operational as both a night bomber and maritime warfare aircraft in the Middle East/Mediterranean theatre. It also enjoyed success in the bomber role in Southeast Asia through to VJ-Day. However, the aircraft's operations in Coastal Command, and in the Middle and Far East theatres lie outside the scope of this book.

This Combat Aircraft volume chronicles the history of the Wellington and the units that operated it during the aircraft's service with RAF Bomber Command, and in from its conception as an Air Staff specification in 1931 through to its final operational sortie with No 300 (Polish) Sqn

A fine study of the first production Wellington I L4212 in flight (*BAE Systems courtesy of Brooklands Museum*)

in March 1944. The book also details the employment of the Wellington as the principal type used by the Operational Training Units (OTUs) of Bomber Command right up to war's end. From equipping just seven squadrons in Bomber Command, plus three OTUs, at the start of World War 2, the Wellington was in service with 22 frontline squadrons (plus others in Coastal Command and in the Middle East) by the end of 1941. Three years later, the RAF still had 22 Wellington-equipped OTUs, each of which was equivalent in aircraft numbers to four operational squadrons.

Much is made of the 'geodetic' structure of the Wellington, but while it was indeed a ground-breaking technique in its day, geodetic design proved to be a technological dead end. In fact, the Wellington was the last bomber to be built using a fabric-covered framework, with later types being constructed entirely of metal using a stressed skin structure. Thus, the Wellington represents, in many ways, the ultimate development of the first generation of monoplane bomber aircraft.

However, the original design incorporated plenty of room for growth, which, coupled with improvements in engine technology, enabled the airframe to keep up with developments in aerial warfare. The Wellington I of 1939 was powered by 965 hp Bristol Pegasus XVIII engines and had a maximum take-off weight of 27,000 lbs. Four years later, equivalent figures for the Wellington X were 1615 hp Bristol Hercules VI engines and a maximum take-off weight of 36,500 lbs – an impressive increase of more than four tons in the same airframe.

The Wellington was blessed with benign handling characteristics by the standards of the day, and its rugged structure proved to be able to withstand considerable damage. These two attributes made the aircraft

A planform view of a Wellington I in flight. The geodetic structure is evident under the skin of the wings, as are the longerons used to attach the fabric skin to the fuselage (*BAE Systems courtesy of Brooklands Museum*)

ideal both as a night bomber and as an operational trainer. They also endeared the Wellington to its crews. Interestingly, the Wellington always had an international flavour to its service. At the beginning of the war the aircraft and crews of the 'New Zealand Squadron' were integrated into Bomber Command – the unit had been training up on the Wellington in Britain when Germany invaded Poland. Over the next few years the Wellington was also used to equip one Czechoslovakian, four Polish, three Australian and no less than 11 Canadian squadrons within Bomber Command.

A series of disastrous daylight raids early in the war emphasized the vulnerability of RAF bomber types, including the Wellington, to fighter attack. Nevertheless, crews displayed great courage and tenacity in continuing to fly daylight sorties until Bomber Command switched to a night campaign in 1940. The Wellington proved to be a better bombing platform than either of its contemporaries, the Armstrong Whitworth Whitley and the Handley Page Hampden, and the number of Wellington units slowly increased until it equipped the majority of Bomber Command squadrons in 1941–42.

During this time, it was primarily the Wellington that gave Britain and its allies the ability to take the offensive into the Third Reich itself. Wellington crews attacked the German industrial heartland in the Ruhr Valley, as well as oil production and storage facilities and naval infrastructure. Considerable effort was expended by Wellington crews against German capital ships while they lay in port in Brest during 1941 and early 1942.

Although the Wellington was gradually supplanted in the frontline by four-engined bombers (Short Stirling, Handley Page Halifax and Avro Lancaster), the aircraft still made up more than half of the entire bomber force that attacked Köln in the first 'thousand-bomber raid' in the summer of 1942. The fact that more than one-third of the Wellingtons that participated in the raid were provided by OTUs reflects the importance of the Wellington as an operational training aircraft.

As Bomber Command continued to expand through late 1942 and into early 1943, many new units, and in particular the Canadian squadrons of No 6 Group, were issued with Wellingtons as a stop-gap until sufficient four-engined 'heavies' became available. The last bomber operation carried out by frontline Wellington squadrons took place in October 1943, although the aircraft remained in frontline service as an aerial mine layer until the spring of 1944. When combat operations ceased, the Wellington continued to train crews in operational techniques right up until the end of hostilities.

Thus, the Wellington played an unmatched and vital part in the bomber offensive, from the opening rounds in 1939 right through to its climax in 1945.

CHAPTER ONE

ORIGINS AND EARLY DAYS

The prototype Vickers B9/32 medium bomber K4049 at Brooklands in 1936. The aircraft was destroyed in a crash at Martlesham Heath on 19 April 1937 (*BAE Systems courtesy of Brooklands Museum*)

The origins of the Wellington lie in the summer of 1931 with forward planning by the Air Staff for a replacement for the Boulton & Paul Sidestrand. By then the biplane bomber, which had entered service with No 101 Sqn just three years earlier, had been overtaken by the rapid advances in aeronautical design and technology and was already obsolete. The formal Air Staff Requirement for a 'multi-engined day bomber' to replace it was issued to the Director of Technical Development at the Air Ministry in October 1931. It specified an aeroplane that could carry a bomb load of 1500 lbs over a range of 720 miles at a speed of 190 mph. The aircraft was to be equipped with three Lewis guns for self-defence and was not to exceed a tare weight (basically the 'unladen' weight) of 6000 lbs, which was a restriction imposed by the Geneva Convention.

Air Ministry Specification B9/32, which was issued for tenders in 1932, stipulated that the new aeroplane was to be a twin-engined day bomber that could carry a load of 'approximately 1 lb per horsepower', made up of 450- or 500-lb bombs, over a normal range of 600 miles at full throttle at 15,000 ft. It required 'good manoeuvrability, a good view for formation flying, for bombing and for night landing, a steady bombing platform with no tendency to "hunt", and fore and aft stability to be unaffected by the release of bombs'. The crew of four would include a pilot and three gunners, one of whom was to be a radio operator, and there was to be a position for the bomb aimer to be seated in the nose of the aircraft.

Two manufacturers successfully tendered for the specification – Vickers (Aviation) Limited, whose Type 271 would evolve into the Wellington, and Handley Page Limited, whose HP 52 would become the Hampden. Both companies concluded that the tare weight restriction was unreasonable and lobbied successfully for it to be relaxed. In fact, the take-off weights of the operational marks of both the Hampden and Wellington easily exceeded 20,000 lbs.

The prototype Vickers aircraft, the Type 271, was designed by the company's chief designer, 'Rex' Pierson, using the Vickers-Wallis System of construction. Also known as the 'geodetic system', this method of construction had been devised by the company's Chief Structural Engineer, Barnes Wallis.

The principle of the geodetic system lies in the behaviour of curved struts bracing a square frame. When subjected to a shear force, an unbraced square frame will tend to deform into a rhombus. Bracing the square across its diagonals will give it more strength – when subjected to the force, one brace will be under tension and the opposite one will be under compression in a different direction. However, the strength of the square will depend on the strength of the braces, and it will still ultimately deform when one strut fails. The geodetic system uses curved, rather than straight, struts as bracing. When the square attempts to deform, the strut under compression will tend to bow outwards while the strut under tension will tend to oppose it by bowing inwards by the same amount. Thus, the shear force is cancelled out. The struts could therefore be smaller and, as a result, a geodetic structure would be much lighter than one using the traditional system of formers and stringers.

Another advantage of this form of construction was that it distributed torsional loads across the whole structure, so if any part of it was damaged, its load would be transferred to the rest of the structure. This particular characteristic meant that the Wellington was able to withstand substantial battle damage without structural failure. The outer skin of the aircraft was made of canvas, which was attached to wooden stringers running the length of the fuselage over the geodetic metal framework.

The Type 271 first flew from the Vickers factory at Brooklands on 15 June 1936. The aircraft, known initially as the Vickers Medium Bomber, was officially christened the Wellington later that year. Unfortunately, the prototype was lost in an accident in 1937, but by then sufficient development work had been done to finalize the configuration of the initial production variant, which was designated the Type 290, or Wellington I.

A total of 178 of these aircraft were built at Weybridge, the Wellington I being powered by two 965 hp Bristol Pegasus XVIII engines driving three-bladed de Havilland propellers. Electrical power was provided by a generator on the starboard engine, while the port engine drove two hydraulic pumps. Each of the latter served a separate system, with the primary powering the undercarriage, flaps and bomb-bay doors and the secondary powering the gun turrets. Two Vickers-built turrets were fitted to the Wellington I, with a 'cupola' in the nose mounting a single Browning 0.303-in machine gun and another in the tail mounting two such guns. In the second half of the production run, provision was made for a retractable ventral turret, although none was actually fitted in the

RIGHT
This photograph of the Wellington I production line at Brooklands in 1938 shows the geodetic structure of the fuselage to good effect. Vickers nose turrets ready for fitting can be seen in the foreground (*BAE Systems courtesy of Brooklands Museum*)

The first production Wellington I L4212 seen at the Aircraft and Armament Experimental Establishment, Martlesham Heath, where it was used for trials during 1938 (*BAE Systems courtesy of Brooklands Museum*)

Mk I. Additionally, in extremis, a hatch in the roof of the fuselage could be used to fire a hand-held weapon.

Fuel tanks in the inner and outer wing panels could be augmented by auxiliary tanks fitted in the forward part of the bomb-bay, giving a range of some 2500 miles. In addition, ungauged reserve fuel tanks, each containing 58 gallons, were located in the engine nacelles. These tanks were operated by cables in the fuselage sides near the wing spar.

The aircraft, which could carry a bomb load of 4500 lbs, was manned by a crew of four – pilot, observer (fulfilling the roles of navigator and bomb aimer), wireless operator and gunner. The crew compartment was heated by a pipe that ran along the length of the fuselage delivering hot air

that had, in turn, been warmed by a steam-heater which derived its heat from the exhaust of the port engine. An inflatable dinghy was housed in the port engine nacelle.

Reports from the Aircraft and Armament Experimental Establishment at Martlesham Heath confirmed that the bomber's handling characteristics were generally benign, although the Wellington did exhibit a tendency to spin if a wing was allowed to drop when the aircraft stalled. The main criticism, however, was the level of noise in the cockpit, which was considered to be extremely fatiguing for the crew. It was also noted that in asymmetric flight (i.e. with an engine throttled back or failed) 'even with bank, rudder trim alone is insufficient to maintain a straight path and a considerable foot load on the rudder control is necessary'. One pilot described the Wellington as 'a docile and friendly thing, very easy to fly (though a bit marginal if one engine failed) and exceptionally easy to land'.

On the take-off run, the aircraft exhibited a very slight tendency to swing to the right, but this was easily controlled with the rudder. To prevent any swing that might be caused by an uneven response from the engines, they were run up to about 1000 rpm before releasing the brakes. Take-off was at about 80 mph and the single-engine safety speed was 120 mph, above which speed the aircraft could be kept straight with the rudder and could climb slowly with the undercarriage retracted. The long-range cruise speed was 160 mph, resulting in a fuel flow of around 40 gallons per hour. The approach speed for an engine-assisted landing was 80 mph, although a speed of 95 mph was needed for a glide approach.

Although the specification B9/32 had been intended to procure a successor to the Sidestrand, that aircraft, which was only operated by No 101 Sqn, was actually replaced by the Bristol Blenheim in 1938. Instead, the Wellington and Hampden were used to replace the Handley Page Heyford and Harrow and the Fairey Hendon medium bombers.

Wellington Is from No 9 Sqn fly in loose formation over the English countryside. Note the large window on the starboard side at the bomb aimer's position (*RAF Museum*)

Detail of the Vickers 'cupola' nose turret as fitted to the Wellington I. In practice, the turret that equipped Mk I aircraft suffered from problems with sighting and proved to be unsuitable (*BAE Systems courtesy of Brooklands Museum*)

The first unit within Bomber Command to operate the Wellington was No 99 Sqn, a Heyford unit based at Mildenhall, which received its first new Mk I on 10 October 1938.

Over the next ten months it was followed by the remaining squadrons in Bomber Command's No 3 Group – No 38 Sqn, based at Marham, converted from the Hendon to the Wellington in November 1938, and both No 149 Sqn at Mildenhall and No 9 Sqn at Stradishall replaced their Heyfords with Wellingtons in January 1939. A second unit at Marham, No 115 Sqn, started its conversion from the Harrow to the Wellington two months later, while No 148 Sqn swapped its Heyfords for Wellingtons as Stradishall at the same time. At Feltwell, Nos 37 and 214 Sqns received Wellingtons in May, and the final re-equipment of Harrow units was completed in July 1938 when Honington-based Nos 75 and 215 Sqns received their Wellingtons.

By this time the group structure of Bomber Command reflected the aircraft types in its inventory, with No 1 Group equipped with Fairey Battles, No 2 Group flying Blenheims, No 3 Group operating Wellingtons, No 4 Group assigned Hampdens and No 5 Group equipped with Whitleys.

As noted in the Introduction, one of the units to receive Wellingtons in the summer of 1939 was the 'New Zealand Squadron', which was staffed by personnel from the Royal New Zealand Air Force (RNZAF). After a major review of the country's defence forces, the New Zealand government had ordered 30 Wellingtons for the newly-formed RNZAF in 1938. The plan was for the aircraft to be taken on charge in Britain so that crews could convert onto the type under RAF supervision. As sufficient numbers of crews became qualified, they would ferry the aircraft to New Zealand in five flights, each of six aircraft.

The first Wellington I, serial number NZ300, was accepted by representatives of the New Zealand government on 27 April 1939. Five more aircraft were delivered in the next month, and all but one of this initial issue of bombers were configured with dual controls for pilot training. The specification of the RNZAF aircraft differed slightly from RAF Wellingtons in the fitting of flotation bags in the bomb-bays and a facility to jettison fuel.

The 'New Zealand Squadron', under the command of Sqn Ldr M W Buckley, began to form at Marham in June 1939. Pilots for the new unit were recruited from amongst the many New Zealanders who were already serving with the RAF, while the remaining crewmen were sent to Britain from New Zealand for training. With the unit formally established, preparations began for the first delivery flight of aircraft to New Zealand, which was planned to set off from England on 1 October 1939.

As the frontline squadrons gained experience in operating the Wellington, the crew complement was increased from four to six, comprising the first pilot/captain, a second pilot, the observer/navigator (who was also responsible for bomb aiming), a wireless operator and two air gunners.

In their routine training, the Wellington squadrons practised bombing on the ranges at Berners Heath (near Bury St Edmunds) and Sutton Bridge/Holbeach (in the Wash) and air-to-air gunnery against towed targets over the Wash. The defensive tactics of the day depended on bombers flying in tight formation so that their armament could provide mutual defence. Experience with Fighter Command's then relatively low performance biplanes and early mark Hurricanes and Spitfires led crews to expect rear quarter attacks, probably from below, which could easily be defeated by the combined firepower from the rear turrets of aircraft in close formation. A beam attack was considered unlikely because the high speed of the Wellington would make the deflection angle too difficult for fighter pilots to judge. In the event of fighter attack, the crew member nominated as 'fire control officer' would man a position in the centre of the aircraft with an intercom connection to all gun positions. Looking through the fuselage windows, he would then direct the turret gunners.

Although the aircraft were to fly in close formation, one tactic involved 'rotating' aircraft whereby Wellingtons flanking the leader swapped sides during the engagement in order to confuse the attacking fighters. In practice, this tactic proved more likely to cause a collision than to hinder enemy aircraft. Eight Wellingtons from No 38 Sqn took part in trials with the Air Fighting Development Establishment between April and July 1939 to investigate tactics for the Wellington. Unfortunately, practice highlighted the shortcomings of the defensive armament of the Wellington and, in particular, the unreliability of the Vickers turrets. The guns were prone to jamming, the rate of traverse was slow and the sighting and aiming mechanism was deemed to be unsuitable. As a result, the Air Ministry instructed Vickers to equip subsequent orders for the aircraft with Nash & Thompson turrets, which were built by Parnall Aircraft Ltd.

Wellington I L4242 of No 38 Sqn on final approach to land. Eight Wellingtons from No 38 Sqn took part in trials with the Air Fighting Development Establishment between April and July 1939 (*RAF Museum*)

Vickers took this opportunity to use the slightly re-designed airframe of the proposed Type 406 Wellington II, which had not yet been produced, to accommodate new turrets. The result was the Type 408 Wellington IA, which began to enter squadron service in late 1939. This variant mounted a two-gun Nash & Thompson FN-5A turret in the nose and another in the tail, and featured a retractable FN-25A ventral turret, which was intended to augment the tail guns. The ventral turret, nicknamed the 'dustbin', could rotate through 360 degrees and fire two degrees above the horizon.

A number of other minor improvements were made to the airframe, including introduction of a fuel jettison system and strengthening the undercarriage to accommodate a higher all-up weight. At the same time, other equipment became standard fit. The Lorenz Blind Landing System, for example, began to be fitted across the fleet, whereas it had previously only been installed in two Mk I aircraft per bomber station.

In addition, the flotation gear used in the RNZAF aircraft was incorporated. This system comprised canvas bags carried in the bomb-bay, which could be inflated by carbon dioxide cylinders. In order to use the flotation gear, it was recommended that all fuel and bomb load be jettisoned. The bomb-bay doors were then closed and the bags inflated. Although the nature of ditching and the possibility of battle damage to the flotation bags made surviving a water landing extremely unpredictable, there is no doubt that the fitting of flotation gear to the Wellington saved the lives of a number of aircrew during the war.

A total of 170 Wellington IAs were built at Weybridge. The possibility of retrospectively modifying the existing Wellington I fleet to the new Mk IA standard was investigated, but it was found to be impractical. Only the last 79 of the 181 Wellington Is built incorporated the structural modifications necessary to fit the ventral turret, and it was not possible to replace the Vickers nose and tail turrets with the Nash & Thompson versions in these particular aircraft – nor would it have been practical to introduce a fuel jettison capability. In any case, by the time that a final decision on the subject was reached in early 1940, it had already been overtaken by events. The Wellington IA was by then about to be replaced by the Mk IC, and the surviving Mk I airframes had already been relegated to training duties.

During the late 1930s, a number of 'shadow' factories were built to supplement aircraft production. A second Vickers-managed factory was constructed at Hawarden, near Chester. Unlike the parent factory at Weybridge, Chester was not intended to produce the aircraft from raw materials. Instead, it was a production line which assembled components that had already been manufactured elsewhere by sub-contractors. Chester started assembling its first batch of Wellingtons in May 1939. Although this run of 100 aircraft had originally been ordered as Mk Is, only three of them were, in fact, completed as such, with 17 built as Mk IAs and the remainder as Mk ICs. Over the next five years, 5540 Wellingtons were built at Chester.

Meanwhile, a third Vickers factory was under construction at Squires Gate, near Blackpool. In view of the vulnerability of Weybridge to air attack, this factory was, unlike the Chester plant, a complete reproduction of the Weybridge facility. It would start Wellington production in September 1940 and eventually build more than 3400 aircraft.

The summer of 1939 was a busy time, with numerous exercises taking place. In a foretaste of the role of Bomber Command in the early part of World War 2, Wellingtons of Nos 9, 115 and 149 Sqns were amongst the bomber units that took part in an exercise against elements of the Home Fleet at anchor in Portland harbour on 25 May. The Wellingtons carried out a simulated attack against the battleships HMS *Rodney* and HMS *Royal Sovereign*, bombing in formation from 15,000 ft. The plan was for all aircraft to release their weapons simultaneously, which, in the case of a real attack, would result in a bomb pattern 500 yards wide and one mile in length. Subsequent analysis by Bomber Command staff indicated that such a largely scattered pattern would be unlikely to obtain hits, an official report stating 'it is considered that the high altitude attack of a ship in harbour is most likely to be successful if bombs are aimed independently by each sub-formation'.

Wellington Is of No 9 Sqn take off from Evere, on the outskirts of Brussels, on 8 July 1939 while participating in the Belgian air force's 25th anniversary air display (*BAE Systems courtesy of Brooklands Museum*)

On 27 June No 149 Sqn consolidated its experience by detaching ten Wellingtons to Tangmere to carry out bombing attacks in the English Channel against HMS *Centurion*, an old Dreadnought battleship that had been converted into a remotely-controlled target ship. Bomber Command regional exercises also took place from 7–13 July. Despite poor weather, three Wellingtons of No 99 Sqn participated in a raid on 7 August. Flying at 500 ft for most of the route because of low cloud, they overflew their target and indicated dropping their weapons by releasing 'Sashalite' flash bulbs. The following day, five aircraft from the same squadron participated in a simulated attack on Salisbury. The poor weather continued during the week, and on 13 July two sub-flights, each comprising a 'vic' of three Wellingtons, carried out raids on Leicester and Cheltenham, respectively. During this sortie, the aircraft flew to their targets from starting points on the east coast of England and, in each case, they were forced at times to fly as low as 50 ft because of the weather.

No 9 Sqn, meanwhile, had been sent to Evere, on the outskirts of Brussels, to represent the RAF at an airshow celebrating the 25th anniversary of the formation of the Belgian air force. The crews led by the squadron commander, Wg Cdr H P Lloyd, arrived in Belgium on the afternoon of 8 July. They were treated to a banquet at the Palais d'Egmont that evening, and the following day they gave a demonstration of formation flying at the airshow. The Wellingtons returned to Stadishall on 13 July, two days before the squadron moved to its new home at Honington. Another 'flag flying' exercise was carried out by nine Wellingtons of No 149 Sqn on 14 July when they took part in the Bastille Day flypast over Paris.

The RAF also carried out a number of long-range training flights over France during July 1939. The Air Ministry was anxious to know what effect a full war load of bombs would have on the tactical range of the aircraft. These flights were designed to check the fuel consumption of a typical operational sortie with a full bomb load, assuming an economical cruise speed to the frontier followed by a maximum cruise speed flight to and from the target and then an economical cruise for the last leg from the frontier back to base.

Six aircraft from No 37 Sqn flew to Bordeaux and back on 11 July and, eight days later, No 9 Sqn led a formation of 18 Wellingtons on an eight-and-a-half-hour flight from Manston to Marseilles and back. For this exercise, the aircraft were drawn from Nos 9, 37, 149 and 214 Sqns. A guest observer in one aircraft on this sortie was Capt H Balfour, the Under-Secretary for Air. The exercise was repeated on 25 July, and the flights provided useful data on fuel consumption when flying long-distance formation sorties. However, all did not go entirely smoothly. During the second flight, two No 9 Sqn Wellingtons, flown by Sqn Ldr R A A Cole and Plt Off H Rosofsky, made force landings at Lyons after in-flight unserviceability.

A maintenance exercise to practice the mobilisation of squadrons commenced at the beginning of August. Personnel were recalled from leave and the aircraft were dispersed and prepared for war. The flying phase started on the 5th, although movements were postponed from the morning because of low cloud and thunderstorms. Instead, an 'exercise injection' of an enemy bombing raid resulted in simulated casualties and damage to aircraft, which all had to be dealt with. At Mildenhall, take-off for the first sortie by No 99 Sqn was at 1530 hrs when Sqn Ldr J F Griffiths, OC 'A' Flight, led aloft three aircraft, each of which dropped a load comprising one 250- and five 500-lb bombs on the range target. Unfortunately, a thunderstorm and cloudburst at Marham prevented No 115 Sqn from taking off. Sorties continued over the next two days, including mixed formations by Nos 99 and 149 Sqns.

The exercise was useful in identifying some shortcomings in wartime procedures. In particular, No 115 Sqn, which was tasked to load nine aircraft each with nine

A formation of Wellington Is of No 149 Sqn, based at Mildenhall, cruise over France. Nine aircraft from the unit took part in the Bastille Day flypast over Paris on 14 July 1939 (*BAE Systems courtesy of Brooklands Museum*)

500-lb bombs and then unload them, reported that 'the procedure takes a disappointing length of time. It is obvious that a considerable increase in armament personnel is required, as unskilled hands, however willing, are dangerous and obstructive'.

The annual Home Defence Air Exercises ran between 8 and 11 August. More than 1300 aircraft were involved in a simulated conflict between 'Westland', represented by the English counties enclosed by the Humber, the Severn and the Solent, and 'Eastland', a fictional continental power equipped with a large air force. Westland was defended by an air force of 500 fighter aircraft and 250 bombers – the latter, which included the Wellingtons of Nos 38, 75, 214 and 215 Sqns, were included to present the Westland defences with a problem of identification. The Wellingtons were tasked to fly 100 miles out to sea before turning back to represent 'friendly' aircraft returning from raids against the enemy. The roundels on the Westland bombers were overpainted with white crosses to identify them as 'friendly forces'.

The attacking force from Eastland comprised 500 bombers, including the Wellingtons of Nos 9, 37, 38, 99, 115 and 149 Sqns, which carried out simulated attacks on targets across Westland. The first wave on 8 August was cancelled because of poor weather, but sorties started in the afternoon and continued through the night. More than 100 raids were flown the following day, despite difficult weather conditions. Unfortunately, Wellington L4258 of No 149 Sqn went missing on the of night 9/10 August and was later reported to have crashed off Happisburgh, killing Flg Off T A Darling and his crew.

The exercise ran for the rest of the week, and on the last night, 10/11 August, London was put under 'black out' conditions. *Flight*'s correspondent H F King flew as an observer in a Wellington mission from Honington that evening and described the experience eloquently in the issue of 17 August;

'The cabin of the "blacked out" Wellington was like the dim nave of a Gothic cathedral. One installed oneself beside the pilot and the big Vickers was soon charging down the flare path and sailing seawards. Lowestoft passed below as we nosed up through ice to 18,000 ft, where we stayed for an asthmatic half-hour, turning south to get into position for the raid. Observation of incidental instruments was done by flashlight, though the navigator occasionally switched on the cabin light. The blowers were now set in high gear.

'As we nosed in north of Southend we were somewhat shaken to see the familiar London glow, though it was, admittedly, subdued. The Estuary water showed up clearly near the lighted buoys, and we saw distinct red lights which we assumed to mark the Dagenham pylons. We were unmistakably over London, though it was difficult to get exact bearings, the lights being in broken masses. We set a slightly southerly course and the searchlights started to grope around us in dozens, so very near and yet so far. The flight lieutenant steered straight for any beam which erected itself ahead, and every time it moved just as we were about to pass into it. But a rising chuckle was squashed by a sudden brilliant illumination of the front turret in which we were now installed and by the sight of another great black Wellington formating a few feet above. I was soon grasping the gun

Wellington I L4341 of No 214 Sqn, based at Methwold, had its roundels overpainted in 'Westland' markings for the annual Home Defence Air Exercises in August 1939 (*BAE Systems courtesy of Brooklands Museum*)

"handlebars" as the flight lieutenant started ducking our ponderous craft through a field of beams, periodically changing the pitch of one Pegasus to "fox" the sound locators. And so we droned on, with stars above and wavering pillars of light below, on course for Newbury. One more light caught us fairly and squarely, but we dodged behind a cloud.

'Of the actual success of our attack we know nothing, but we indicated our run (with) our recognition lights and set off our Sashalites before turning for Bury and the North Sea. As we went, we watched those groping beams criss-crossing the night sky. It seemed like a Hollywood first-night and, somehow, like the Fifth of November. But it was none of these. It was a rehearsal for war, grim and loathsome.'

General mobilisation of the RAF was initiated on 1 September 1939 in anticipation of the declaration of war against Germany in the next few days. A number of units, including two of the No 3 Group Wellington squadrons, were moved to dispersed locations – No 99 Sqn deployed to Newmarket, where it flew from the Rowley Mile on the racecourse, while No 214 Sqn moved to Methwold two days later.

Even as war broke out, the RAF was still in the midst of an expansion scheme, and a large training task remained outstanding. Three Wellington units, Nos 75, 148 and 215 Sqns, were transferred from No 3 Group to No 6 Group as training units. Furthermore, although No 214 Sqn remained in No 3 Group, it became a 'reserve squadron', tasked with operational training for new crews and providing attrition replacement crews and aircraft for the operational units within the group.

Of the units transferred to No 6 Group, both Nos 75 and 148 Sqns moved to Harwell, where the former carried out armament and operational training, while the latter was responsible for conversions to type and navigation training. The remaining training unit, No 215 Sqn, moved to Bassingbourn, where it was joined by the 'New Zealand Squadron'. Personnel from the latter unit had been informed by letter on 28 August that 'in the event of war the New Zealand Squadron is to be placed at the disposal of the Royal Air Force'. The planned delivery to New Zealand on 1 October was cancelled, and instead of preparing for the long flight home, the RNZAF crews began working up for operations against Germany.

CHAPTER TWO

INTO COMBAT

W hen Britain declared war on Germany at 1100 hrs on 3 September 1939, Bomber Command already had a strike force at readiness to attack German warships in the North Sea. A reconnaissance flight on the afternoon of 3 September by a Blenheim of No 139 Sqn located several vessels, but communications difficulties meant that the information did not reach Bomber Command until late in the day.

Six Wellingtons from No 37 Sqn, led by Flt Lt C J S Dickens (L4328), and another three from No 149 Sqn, led by Sqn Ldr H I Dabinett (L4254), took off at around 1830 hrs to attack the shipping. Three more aircraft from No 149 Sqn were due to join them, but they were cancelled before they took off. The nine aircraft found their progress blocked by solid cloud between 1000 ft and 12,000 ft, and in the falling darkness they split off individually, jettisoned their bombs into the sea and returned home.

The following morning, another reconnaissance flight confirmed the continued presence of warships in the Schillig Roads, and in the early afternoon a force of 14 Wellingtons drawn from Nos 9 and 149 Sqns set out to bomb them. Two battleships had been identified near Brünsbuttel, a small port that lies at the entrance of the Kiel Canal in the mouth of the Elbe. The weather was atrocious, with low cloud and poor visibility, and the first three aircraft from No 149 Sqn, led by Flt Lt A G Duguid (L4272), took off at 1445 hrs and quickly ran into difficulties. They jettisoned their weapons and returned to base.

A 'vic' formation of Wellington ICs from No 149 Sqn over East Anglia in August 1940. The nearest aircraft, R3206, was later transferred to No 311 (Czech) Sqn and thence to No 27 OTU (*Philip Jarrett*)

Five more Wellingtons from the squadron, led by Sqn Ldr P I Harris (L4302), took off ten minutes later, and although Sgts Hayes (L4271) and Harrison (L4263) lost formation and returned to base, Sqn Ldr Harris, Flg Off W J Macrae (L4265) and Flt Sgt J B Stewart (L4229) pressed on to the Elbe estuary. Flg Off Macrae bombed Brünsbuttel, but Sqn Ldr Harris and Flt Sgt Stewart dropped their ordnance in the sea near Tönning and Cuxhaven, respectively.

The six aircraft from No 9 Sqn were from 4 Section, led by Flt Lt I P Grant, which took off at 1540 hrs, and 1 Section, led by Sqn Ldr L S Lamb, which followed 20 minutes later. Despite the appalling weather conditions, Flt Lt Grant (L4278) and Sgts T Purdie (L4287) and C Bowen (L4262), flying at 600 ft, found a battleship south of the entrance to the Kiel Canal and bombed it. 'Immediately after release', reported Grant, 'we were forced to pull into cloud owing to the very high concentration of anti-aircraft fire'.

Unfortunately, by the time 1 Section reached the target area, flying at 400 ft, the defences had been fully alerted and the Wellingtons were intercepted by nine Luftwaffe fighters. Sqn Ldr Lamb (L4329) managed to locate the harbour area despite being under attack, and later reported;

'I jettisoned my three bombs "live and in stick" in the south side of the harbour. At the moment of bombing I felt sure there was no shipping in the vicinity, but having pressed the bomb release I saw a merchant ship. It was necessary for the safety of my crew that these bombs were jettisoned, as the decreased load enabled the machine to successfully evade the attack.'

Lamb pulled up into the low cloud base and was able to escape his attackers and return to Honington. However, his wingmen were less fortunate, with the aircraft of Flt Sgts I E M Burley (L4268) and A J Turner (L4275) both being shot down.

The defensive firepower of the Wellington squadrons was improved with the arrival of the Wellington IA equipped with Nash & Thompson gun turrets, which started to reach operational units in early September. No 9 Sqn received its first Mk IA on 6 September, with No 99 Sqn following suit three weeks later. The new variant was enthusiastically received, with the OC of No 99 Sqn commenting that 'the Mk IA Wellington with FN turrets allows far better firing results than the Mk I with Vickers turrets'. When No 149 Sqn received its first Wellington IA, the unit carried out a performance trial and found that with a full bomb load of 1500 lbs, full tanks with

A close-up view of the two-gun Nash & Thompson FN-5A turret fitted in the tail of the Wellington IA, IC, IV and, as shown here, the Mk II (*BAE Systems courtesy of Brooklands Museum*)

720 gallons, a crew of five and full operational equipment, the aircraft took off in 1080 yards. It could climb to 20,000 ft, but at this altitude the Wellington was 'very sluggish and wallowed considerably'. Over the course of the next few months, the Mk I was phased out of service and replaced by the Mk IA in all frontline units.

The first wartime mission undertaken by No 99 Sqn was flown on 8 September. Four aircraft were to proceed independently to carry out a reconnaissance of Wilhelmshaven and Bremen and then to drop leaflets over Hanover. The leaflets were codenamed 'Nickels', and leaflet dropping became known as 'nickelling'. The lead aircraft, flown by Sqn Ldr J F Griffiths, was unserviceable, but the remaining three bombers flown by Flt Sgts J S Brent (L4225) and W H Downey (R2701) and Sgt A Helmsley (L4309) set off for Germany that evening. Brent had to abort when a stack of leaflets that were being stored in the cabin fell from their stowage and jammed the aileron controls. Downey and Helmsley carried out their missions, but an unexpectedly strong westerly wind made navigation uncertain and both aircraft ended up short of fuel and diverted to Manston. Helmsley's aircraft had only 40 gallons remaining, and its tailplane was found to have been hit and damaged by a bundle of leaflets.

Throughout the autumn a strike force was kept at readiness to attack the German fleet when an opportunity presented itself. In addition, Wellington units carried out periodic armed reconnaissance 'sweeps' of the North Sea in search of enemy naval forces. If such vessels were located, they were to be attacked 'from no lower than 2000 ft'.

An armed reconnaissance was flown by nine aircraft from No 99 Sqn and a further nine from No 149 Sqn on the afternoon of 30 October in response to reports of German warships off Terschelling. Once again the weather was unhelpful, with a solid cloud base at 2000 ft, and despite an extensive search in the gathering dusk no enemy shipping was found. The main problem for the formation was how to recover 18 aircraft that arrived overhead at Mildenhall almost simultaneously in the darkness. It was nearly an hour between the first and last aircraft landing.

On 3 December 24 Wellingtons from Nos 9, 38, 115 and 149 Sqns set out to attack warships off Heligoland. The formation, which was led by OC No 149 Sqn, Wg Cdr R Kellett (N2960), formed up over Thetford before routing through clear skies towards their objective. Broken cloud had formed over the target at about 7000 ft, but there were enough gaps in the cloud to allow crews to identify two cruisers sheltering between the islands and bomb them. They did not manage to score any hits, and the formation successfully fought off, without loss, a few fighters that attempted to intercept them. Although no damage had been achieved by the raid, the mission was considered to be a successful demonstration of how a large bomber force could fight its way to and from a target.

On 14 December, despite a low cloud base of 600–1000 ft, a number of sweeps were made during the course of the day by Nos 9, 37, 38, 99, 115 and 149 Sqns. The patrol by No 99 Sqn took place in the early afternoon, with 12 Wellingtons (a mix of Mk Is and Mk IAs) being led by Sqn Ldr Griffiths. The formation comprised six aircraft in two vics (1 and 2 Sections) in trail, with another six aircraft in two vics (3 and 4 Sections, led by Sqn Ldr R G R Catt) 200 yards behind the first section and offset

A rare photograph of Wellington IAs from No 9 Sqn with ventral 'dustbin' turrets extended. The turrets, which could rotate through 360 degrees and fire two degrees above the horizon, were used routinely to augment the defensive firepower during daylight operations in the early months of the war (*Philip Jarrett*)

to the right. After patrolling the sea between Heligoland and Wangerooge, the easternmost Frisian Island, where cloud was as low as 300 ft in places, the Wellington formation encountered a German battleship escorted by destroyers and flak ships at around 1425 hrs. The Wellingtons were unable to attack because of the low cloud base, and they were engaged by anti-aircraft fire and subjected to a concerted attack by Bf 109 and Bf 110 fighters.

Although the unit kept good formation, five Wellingtons were shot down and, as a Bomber Command report of the mission later recorded, 'all fighter attacks were made from astern and generally above, so that the "dustbins" [ventral turrets] could not be brought to bear'. One of the first casualties was Flt Lt N L Lewis (N2870) in the first section. Unfortunately, when he dropped back after being damaged, his aircraft collided with that of Flt Sgt W H Downey (N2991), who was following close behind in 2 Section, and both aircraft crashed. Flt Sgt J E K. Healey (N2886) in 2 Section was also shot down and 4 Section was badly mauled, losing two aircraft (Flg Off J A H Cooper in N2936 and Sgt R H J Brace in N2986) during the action and the section leader (Flt Lt E J Heatherington in N2957), who crashed near Newmarket. Thus, the formation had lost 50 per cent of its strength to enemy action.

Despite this, Bomber Command staff officers stuck to the pre-war mantra that 'the maintenance of tight, unshakeable, formations in the face of the most powerful enemy action is the test of the bomber force fighting efficiency and morale. In our Service it is the equivalent of the old "Thin Red Line" or the "Shoulder to Shoulder" of Cromwell's Ironsides'. However, it must have been clear even at this early stage of the war that the tactic of using unescorted bombers in daytime was fatally flawed. Nevertheless, daylight raids continued.

On 18 December Wg Cdr Kellett once again led a formation of 24 Wellingtons from Nos 9, 37 and 149 Sqns to attack enemy warships in the Schilling Roads and in Wilhelmshaven. To an extent, Kellett had been handed a poisoned chalice. Indeed, Flg Off P I Harris later recalled that Kellett 'had never had the chance to practise formation flying and bombing with the leaders of Nos 9 or 37 Sqns, to impose his will on them, or formulate any plan for bombing and fighting either as a Group or by Squadrons or by Flights, or to discuss our tactics in the face of fighter attack'.

The formation was flown in a stepped up 'box' of four sub-formations, each made up of six aircraft. The first sub-formation comprised No 149 Sqn, the second, stepped up by 500 ft on the leader's right, was led by Harris (N2980) and consisted of a section each from Nos 9 and 149 Sqns, the third, on the leader's left, was made up from No 9 Sqn, and the fourth, stepped up 1000 ft above and behind the leader, was filled by No 37 Sqn. Harris noted that 'No 37 Sqn were flying in pairs, not vic formation of three like the rest of us, but in line astern, stepped down; it was more manoeuvrable, but had obvious disadvantages since the rear guns could shoot down their own people'. Two aircraft dropped out from the lead formation with engine trouble shortly after coasting out, but the remaining 22 aircraft continued over the North Sea at 14,000 ft. Having found nothing in Heligoland Bight, Kellett led his formation to Wilhelmshaven, where the Wellingtons were greeted with heavy flak. Unfortunately, they were unable to bomb the docks because the rules of engagement at that stage of the war prevented them from doing so.

As the Wellington formation left the target area, it was engaged by a strong force of Bf 109s and Bf 110s. The unwieldy formation broke down and the German fighters pounced on the opportunity as the bombers lost their defensive cross-cover. The rear section of No 37 Sqn aircraft was decimated, with Sqn Ldr I V Hue-Williams (N2904), Flg Offs A T Thompson (N2935), P A Wimberley (N2888) and O J T Lewis (N2889) and Sgt H Ruse (N2936) all being shot down. The only surviving aircraft from this section, flown by Flg Off P C Lemon (N2903), had left the formation near Wilhelmshaven after the pilot inadvertently operated the flap controls. Lemon descended rapidly to sea-level and fought off two Bf 109s, one of which was downed by the tail gunner, Cpl Kidd. N2903 was the only one to survive from the Number 4 formation.

The Number 3 formation was also badly mauled, with the leader, Sqn Ldr A J Guthrie (N2872), as well as Flg Offs D B Allison (N2941), J T I Challes (N2939) and E. F. Lines (N2940) being shot down. The remaining two aircraft, flown by Sgt F C Petts (N2873) and Flg Off W J Macrae (N2871), were badly damaged and force landed at Sutton Bridge and North Coates, respectively.

In the Number 2 formation, Harris 'kept as close to Kellett as possible and Grant clung to me like a limpet, flying really well. So, our nine aircraft presented a concentrated but unattractive target, with nine rear turrets and nine "dustbins" to contend with. My second pilot, Flg Off Sandy Innes, a splendid Scotsman, was at the astrodome to control the gunners. This he did magnificently like a commentator at a football match, so I knew what was going on. Sgt Watson, my navigator, manned the dustbin'.

Wellington IA N2873 of No 9 Sqn at Sutton Bridge, showing the battle damage it incurred during the ill-fated raid on Wilhelmshaven on 18 December 1939 (*RAF Museum*)

The formation fought its way home, but two of the aircraft in the Number 2 formation, flown by Sgt J R Ramshaw (N2983) and Flg Off M F Briden (N2961) were so badly damaged that they ditched in the sea. While Ramshaw's crew was rescued, all of Briden's crew perished. The four aircraft in the leading formation were not immune to attack, with Flg Off J H C Speirs (N2962) being shot down in flames over Wilhelmshaven.

Of the 22 Wellingtons that reached Heligoland, only ten made it back, of which at least two were heavily damaged. Commenting on the debacle, Gp Capt H P Lloyd, the former pre-war OC of No 9 Sqn, wrote 'I have led No 3 Group personally on a number of occasions, and on each I have had a good deal to say about the rear formations. I have also led the rear formation, and I could only keep it together by considering my formation as quite separate. If I tried to catch up with the rest it led to straggling, and I gave it up. It is impossible to cut corners and catch up because leading a formation of Wellingtons is like driving an Austin 7 with a three-ton caravan behind and a good steep downhill in front with some hairpin corners'. Lloyd concluded that 'all four formations of six each should have been entirely separate, with no restriction as to mutual support'.

Amongst other recommendations which came from reviewing the sortie was that self-sealing tanks should be fitted to the Wellington as a matter of urgency and that a gun should be mounted in the astrodome.

'Nickelling' sorties by individual aircraft continued at night time throughout the first months of 1940. Leaflets were dropped on the cities of Bremen, Hamburg and Hanover. Apart from maintaining standby for operations against warships of the Kriegsmarine, squadrons carried out routine training, including fighter affiliation with Spitfire and Hurricane units, bombing practice on various ranges and air-to-air firing against towed sleeve targets. Routine daytime sweeps over the North Sea by smaller formations also continued.

On 2 January 18 aircraft in sections of three from Nos 9, 38, 115 and 149 Sqns carried out six sweeps. Wellingtons from No 9 Sqn, led by Sqn Ldr E P Hutton (N2898), took off at 1100 hrs, but reported seeing nothing of importance. Three aircraft from No 149 Sqn, led by Flg Off H L M Bulloch (N2943), departed at midday, and by about 1400 hrs they were 80 miles west of Heligoland heading south. Suddenly they were bounced by 12 Bf 110s that attacked out of the sun. Taken by surprise, the formation became slightly stretched, enabling a Bf 110 to cut into the formation and shoot down Bulloch's Wellington.

In the No 2 position, Plt Off H A Innes (N2828) had noticed Bulloch rocking his wings as a sign of impending fighter attack, but he did not see the Bf 110s until they opened fire. His ventral turret gunner, Sgt Austin, saw a burst of gunfire come through the fuselage and he immediately lowered his turret and opened fire in return. The rear gunner, AC1 Mullineaux, meanwhile, had already engaged the enemy. The No 3 aircraft, flown by Sgt J Morrice (N2946), was also hit and started to dive steeply away. Innes attempted to follow, but despite reaching 300 mph he could not catch up. Shortly afterwards Morrice's aircraft crashed into the sea. Innes stated that he 'had come to the conclusion that in a dive, the under turret becomes a rear gun and has got another 20–30 degrees of extra range-of-fire, thus cutting out attack from above'. He descended to 20 ft above the sea, retracted the ventral turret and headed for home. Although Innes was chased by five fighters, he managed to evade them.

As a result of this action, HQ No 3 Group instructed that ventral turrets were to be lowered ready for action as aircraft crossed the 4th meridian east.

Periodic sweeps continued through the next two months, but no contact was made with German naval forces. However, after warships were reported off Heligoland on 20 February, the Wellingtons of Nos 37, 38, 99, 115 and 149 Sqns were tasked with bombing them that night. Unfortunately, none of the aircraft could locate the target because of poor weather, and fog at Mildenhall on their return meant that bombers from Nos 99 and 149 Sqns had to divert to various airfields in Lincolnshire.

Flg Off R M Curtis (pilot), Plt Off R M Sanderson (second pilot) and Sgts McMaster (navigator), T J Goodhue (wireless operator), Beckett (front gunner) and J N Richie (rear gunner) of No 75 (NZ) Sqn pose with 'Cuthbert the skeleton' painted on Wellington IA L7848 (*Wellington Aviation*)

The 'New Zealand Squadron' moved to Feltwell and commenced operations in March, starting with a sweep by two aircraft on 10 March. The first 'nickelling' sorties by the unit were flown by three aircraft on 27 March. In the meantime, changes within the training organization at No 6 Group led to the disbandment of Nos 75, 148 and 215 Sqns. However, on 4 April, the No 75 Sqn 'number plate' was passed on to the 'New Zealand Squadron'. At the end of April No 148 Sqn was reformed at Stradishall, only to be disbanded again a month later.

Amid concerns over German designs on Scandinavia, 12 aircraft each from Nos 9 and 115 Sqns were temporarily seconded to No 18 Group Coastal Command and deployed to Lossiemouth and Kinloss, respectively, on 2 April. A naval observer was added to each crew and the aircraft were tasked with keeping a continuous watch over Bergen, Kristiansand and Stavanger. These sorties involved an over-sea leg of 300 miles, adding to the challenges of navigation in poor spring weather.

On the afternoon of 7 April, a Coastal Command aircraft reported the presence of the battlecruisers *Scharnhorst* and *Gneisenau* in the North Sea, although a sweep by a combined force of 12 aircraft from Nos 9 and 115 Sqns could not locate them in the poor visibility. German forces invaded Denmark and Norway two days later, and once again a formation of 12 Wellingtons from the two squadrons set out, this time to attack the cruisers *Köln* and *Köningsberg*, which had been reported at Bergen. The aircraft bombed their targets but no hits were scored on either ship.

Wellington I L4387, flown by Flt Lt A A N Breckon of No 75 (NZ) Sqn, took off from Wick on 12 April to carry out a reconnaissance of the Norwegian coast as far north as Narvik. For this mission, the aircraft had been fitted with long-range fuel tanks. After a successful reconnaissance, the bomber returned to Wick after a flight lasting 14½ hrs.

That same day, British forces landed at Namsos and *Scharnhorst* was located again, accompanied by a cruiser, steaming 100 miles south of Stavanger. During the course of the 12th, Wellingtons and Hampdens of Bomber Command attempted to intercept the enemy warships, with nine aircraft from No 9 Sqn, led by Sqn Ldr Peacock (P9232), taking off at 0925 hrs. Once off Norway they encountered snow and ice, with a cloud base down to 400 ft in places, and were unable to find the target. The aircraft of Sgt C R Bowen (P2520) failed to return. Around midday, another eight Wellingtons from No 37 Sqn, in company with four more from No 75 (NZ) Sqn, were also unsuccessful.

In a third attempt, during the early afternoon, 12 Wellingtons, comprising six each from Nos 38 and 149 Sqns, also failed to find the ships, although they were intercepted by German fighters near Stavanger. In the ensuing running fight, the No 38 Sqn aircraft of Sqn Ldr M Nolan (P9269) was shot down, as were two bombers from No 149 Sqn. In the first minutes of the engagement, the No 149 Sqn aircraft had become separated from the No 38 Sqn formation and the second section overtook the first. In the confusion, Sgt H J Wheller (P9246) nearly rammed his leader, then left the formation and was last seen heading towards the Norwegian coast at low level. The formation descended to sea level in an attempt to escape, but Sgt G E Goad (P9266) was downed. Six Hampdens were also lost to enemy fighters that day.

Over the next fortnight, Bomber Command aircraft attempted to support the ground forces at Namsos and Åndalsnes by raiding Norwegian airfields occupied by the Luftwaffe. Many were beyond the range of the bombers, but Stavanger and Kristiansand, as well as Aalborg, in Denmark, could be reached. Just after dusk on 17 April, Wellingtons from Nos 37, 75 (NZ) and 99 Sqns, each configured with overload tanks and four 250-lb bombs, set out for Stavanger. One of three Wellingtons from No 75 (NZ) Sqn had to return to base with an electrical problem, but Flg Offs J N Collins (P9207) and N Williams (P9212) bombed the airfield successfully. Unfortunately, Flg Off A F Smith (P9234) of No 99 Sqn failed to return to base.

Mid-April 1940 saw the introduction into service of the Vickers Type 416 Wellington IC, which had been shaped by operational experiences gained during the first months of the war. The Mk IC began to replace the Mk IA in frontline units from this date. Some 2685 Wellington ICs were built, as compared to just 180 of each of the Mk I and Mk IA versions and around 1450 each of the Hampden and Whitley, making it the most important aircraft type in Bomber Command during the early war years.

The new variant featured a redesigned hydraulic system and incorporated a 24-volt electrical system, which was needed to power the directional radio compass. The traverse arc of the front turret was also increased by cutting away the forward fuselage immediately behind it. This modification (which was incorporated from R3150 onwards in the production line) increased the field of fire of the turret by 18 degrees, enabling the nose guns to fire onto the beam. Perhaps the most fundamental change was the decision taken in June 1940 to delete the ventral turret. The switch to night operations had made it redundant, and removing the 800-lb turret would allow a heavier bombload to be carried. However, No 3 Group staff had pointed out that aircraft taking off in darkness might return to base in the morning twilight when they could be vulnerable to fighters. Learning from the lessons of early raids, it was considered that beam guns (Vickers K machine guns firing through the fuselage cabin windows above the wing) should be fitted in lieu of the ventral turret.

On the night of 20/21 April, six aircraft from No 37 Sqn led by Sqn Ldr R L Bradford (P9213) attacked Kristiansand airfield and three Wellingtons from No 149 Sqn, led by Wg Cdr Kellett (P9224), attacked Aalborg. Meanwhile, Sqn Ldr Jarman (P9239) led six aircraft from No 9 Sqn and another six from No 99 Sqn to bomb Stavanger, where they found the target obscured by cloud. Flt Lt T S Rivett-Carnac (P9231) of No 9 Sqn managed to find and bomb the airfield, but none of the other crews could do so – Flt Sgt Snowden (P9257) of No 99 Sqn spent 90 minutes in the target area attempting unsuccessfully to find it and ran so short of fuel that he had to divert to Leuchars.

The following night Aalborg was revisited at ten-minute intervals by three aircraft from No 75 (NZ) Sqn and a further bomber from No 149. Sqn Ldr W I Collett (P9248) and Flg Off F T Knight (P9218) from No 149 Sqn made their attack from low level, but Knight was shot down by the ground defences and crash-landed at Limfjorden, where his crew was captured. The same night, six aircraft from No 38 Sqn attacked Stavanger, where they reported intensive anti-aircraft fire.

Westerland airfield, on the island of Sylt, was bombed by Nos 9, 37 and 115 Sqns on the night of 23 April. Flt Lt Fordham (P9278), leading the six aircraft, from No 9 Sqn reported 'intense searchlight activity was reported on the island of Sylt that considerably reduced the accuracy of bombing. A considerable amount of light flak and heavy AA fire was met over the vicinity of the target'. Two nights later, six aircraft from No 149 Sqn, led by Flt Lt I D Grant-Crawford (P9270), and six from No 99 Sqn set out to bomb Stavanger airfield once more, but after flying through difficult icing conditions, they were unable to identify the target because of cloud cover.

At the end of April, British forces started to withdraw from Norway and Bomber Command resumed its attacks on local airfields to cover the evacuation. Two Wellingtons from No 37 Sqn's 'A' Flight (Sqn Ldr Bradford (P9213) and Flg Off G V Gordon (P9215)) and two from 'B' Flight (Sgt Fletcher (N2992) and Flg Off Warner (P7779)) bombed Stavanger airfield on the evening of 30 April, operating in two pairs. It was still light when first pair attacked from south to north and the second from east to west. The aircraft then descended to low level to egress from the target area.

However, they were intercepted by enemy fighters that had been scrambled during the attack and a force of four Bf 109s and two Bf 110s chased the leading pair. The second pair, in trail behind Bradford and Gordon and zig-zagging at 210 mph at low level, was also engaged by Bf 109s. A running fight continued between sea

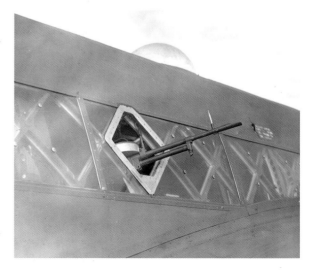

A detail view of the initial fitting of the Vickers K 0.303-in 'beam gun' in the Wellington IC. This mounting was eventually replaced with a Browning 0.303-in machine gun mounted further aft in the fuselage (*BAE Systems courtesy of Brooklands Museum*)

'Bombing up' a Wellington IC of No 149 Sqn at Mildenhall with 250 lb General Purpose (GP) bombs. The Wellington could carry a maximum bomb load of 4500 lbs (*BAE Systems courtesy of Brooklands Museum*)

level and 500 ft for the next 30 minutes, during which one Bf 109 was shot down by the rear pair. Bradford and Gordon both had their ventral turrets in use, but to no avail, and they were shot down. The rear pair had decided to retract their turrets in order to gain more speed and both of these aircraft returned safely.

Taking off an hour later that same evening, six Wellingtons from No 99 Sqn, three from No 9 Sqn and six from No 115 Sqn joined up over Wells, also bound for Stavanger. The lead aircraft from No 99 Sqn suffered an engine failure, so Flt Sgt Brent (P9276) took over as leader. The Wellingtons continued in vee-formations to Stavanger, where they found the target thanks to a bright fire burning to the southeast of the airfield. The formations split into individual aircraft in order to make their bombing runs in gentle dives from 9000 ft down to 7000 ft before returning to base independently. Despite the efforts of the target defences, the only casualty was Flg Off Gibbs (R3154), who crashed on the North York Moors while attempting to descend below cloud during the transit home.

The final raid on Stavanger by Wellingtons was made on the night of 7/8 May when three aircraft each from Nos 37, 38, 115 and 75 (NZ) Sqns were detailed to bomb the airfield – it was completely obscured by cloud and they were unable to pinpoint the target.

By now, No 3 Group was tasking its Wellington units by station wings, rather than directly by squadron, so, for example, targets allocated to Marham would be met equally by Nos 38 and 115 Sqns and targets allocated to Feltwell would be met by Nos 37 and 75 (NZ) Sqns.

After their successes in Denmark and Norway, the Germans invaded the Low Countries on 10 May. Paratroopers seized Waalhaven airfield in Rotterdam early in the morning, and at the request of the Dutch authorities, Blenheims of No 600 Sqn were tasked with attacking the airfield. That evening follow-up attacks were carried out by 36 Wellingtons, comprising three aircraft each from Nos 37 and 75 (NZ) Sqns and six each from Nos 9, 38, 99, 115 and 149 Sqns. It was a dark night with no moon, but the weather was good and all of the aircraft found their targets easily because of the large fires burning in the vicinity. The first three from No 9 Sqn took off just after 1900 hrs and proceeded to the target area in formation, led by Sqn Ldr G E Peacock (P9232), but subsequent aircraft left singly in a 10–15-minute stream. Two of the No 9 Sqn bombers were damaged by anti-aircraft fire, but all of the Wellingtons returned home safely.

The invasion of Belgium and the Netherlands triggered bombing attacks on the oil and steel industries in Germany itself. On the night of 12/13 May, Wellingtons from Nos 37 and 75 (NZ) Sqns attacked industrial targets in Krefeld, and the following night Nos 99 and 149 Sqns targeted Aachen. However, these were not concentrated attacks, and from a squadron strength of between six and 12 aircraft, a number of different targets would be specified for every two to four bombers. On the night of 15/16 May, the strengths of Nos 38 and 115 Sqns were stretched across targets at Duisburg, Homberg and Gelsenkirchen, while those of Nos 37 and 75 (NZ) Sqns attacked Aachen, Oberhausen and Turnhout.

During the second half of May, operations in support of the army in France became the targeting priority for Bomber Command. Nearly every night from the 17th until the final withdrawal from Dunkirk on 5 June, Wellington squadrons attacked various tactical targets and attempted to interdict road and rail traffic in Belgium. The wings were tasked on alternate nights, and most squadrons were able to launch 11 or 12 aircraft. For example, Nos 9 and 115 Sqns each sent 12 bombers to the Cambrai area, and on 20 and 21 May Nos 37, 75 (NZ), 99 and 149 Sqns attacked road and rail targets in the Namur-Dinant area. On 22 May it was the turn of Nos 9, 38 and 115 Sqns again, this time attacking transport infrastructure and troop concentrations, and on 23 May Nos 37, 38, 75 (NZ), 99, 115 and 149 Sqns bombed similar targets. Small-scale raids on Germany continued in late May, but it was not until June that the campaign against the oil and steel facilities recommenced, albeit at a lesser pace than the operations to support the army in France.

At this stage of the war, the German night defences were relatively ineffective, and there were very few losses amongst the Wellington crews. Nevertheless, Plt Off D W W Morris (R3152) and Flt Sgt L G Moores (P9298), both from No 115 Sqn, failed to return from a sortie on the night of 21/22 May by ten aircraft from the unit and another ten from No 38 Sqn against road traffic in the Cambrai–St Quentin area. That night No 75 (NZ) Sqn also suffered its first combat loss when Flt Lt J N Collins (R3157) failed to return from a mission to Aachen, and on 5/6 June, Sqn Ldr Peacock (P9232) of No 9 Sqn was downed over Duisburg during a raid by 12 Wellingtons from the unit against targets in the Ruhr valley. That same night No 37 Sqn lost Plt Off W A Gray (L7791) over Cambrai during operations against a nearby transportation target and the marshalling yards at Mönchen-Gladbach.

Wellington squadrons were also involved in an unconventional campaign during June 1940 when Bomber Command attempted to start large-scale forest fires in Germany. Operation *Razzle* involved dropping small packets of inflammable celluloid – 'Razzles' – packed around a piece of phosphorous wrapped in wet cotton wool. The principle of the weapon was that as the cotton wool dried out, the phosphorous would spontaneously ignite and, in turn, set the celluloid aflame. 'Razzles' were dropped over the Black Forest by Nos 9, 37 and 75 (NZ) Sqns on the night of 7/8 June, and a larger 'Razzle' mission took place on the night of 14/15 June involving aircraft from Nos 99, 149, 38, 115, 9, 37, 75 (NZ) and 214 Sqns. The 'Razzle' proved to be an ineffective weapon.

Italy declared war on Britain on 10 June, and the next day Whitleys of No 6 Group bombed Turin. Six Wellingtons from both Nos 37 and 75

A Wellington IC of No 214 Sqn is pulled into a hangar at Stradishall for maintenance work. The unit changed its code letters from the pre-War 'UX' to 'BU' belatedly in 1940 (*Graham Pitchfork*)

(NZ) Sqns also deployed to Salon, in southern France, on 11 June, but they did not carry out any sorties over Italy because of political pressure from the French government. However, another 12 Wellingtons, this time from Nos 99 and 149 Sqns and led by Sqn Ldr D. A. Kerr (P9248), flew to Salon on the morning of 15 June. That night they bombed the Ansaldo works and an aluminium plant at Genoa. The next night they attacked the Caproni works in Milan. The aircraft returned home on 17 June.

Missions over Germany continued through July and August, typically with each squadron providing six aircraft for operations on alternate nights. Targeting was still not concentrated. For example, on 14/15 July, No 37 Sqn was tasked with sending four Wellingtons against the docks at Hamburg and five aircraft against the marshalling yards at Hamm, while No 75 (NZ) Sqn sent seven aircraft against three different targets. That night, two of the No 75 Sqn crews saw Sgt J F McCauley (L7792) of No 37 Sqn downed in flames over Bremen.

On 17 August No 37 Sqn sent eight Wellingtons against three targets – four to the oil refinery at Zeitz, near Leipzig, two to the marshalling yards at Soest and two to the Schwerte marshalling yards near Dortmund. Plt Off Hough (L7780) could not locate the refinery and headed home with his bombs still on board. About 50 miles off Yarmouth on the return leg, the Wellington was attacked by a Bf 110 nightfighter. He reported that 'at the time of the attack the Wellington was silhouetted against the moon. The ME110 (sic) attacked from the port quarter, firing with his front gun, the bullets passing approximately six feet under the main plane. He crossed astern and on coming on to the beam he fired a short burst with the dorsal gun. The rear gunner, Sgt McDermid, observed this attack developing and opened fire from a range of 200 yards until the enemy was masked by the tailplane. To enable the rear gunner to keep the enemy in his sights for a longer period, the Captain turned to port. As the ME110 came around to the front of the Wellington, the Captain dived in an attempt to render the dorsal gun ineffective. During this manoeuvre the front gunner did not have a chance to fire. The ME110 then came around to deliver a second attack from the port quarter. As he closed in to attack Sgt McDermid opened fire at a range of 100–150 yards. Incendiary bullets were seen to strike the engine and the enemy aircraft went into a dive with smoke and sparks coming from it.'

The first raid against Berlin was mounted on the night of 25/26 August by Nos 99 and 149 Sqns. The latter unit's eight Wellingtons were led by Sqn Ldr D. F. Kerr (P9268) against Templehof aerodrome. Two nights later Nos 149 and 214 Sqns attacked *Gneisenau* in Kiel harbour. Flt Lt P F R Vaillant (P9272) failed to return from this sortie. Berlin was revisited on the night of 30/31 August by Nos 99, 149 and 214 Sqns, and again on the following night by Nos 38 and 115 Sqns.

Aircrew represented the frontline of a bomber squadron, but operational flying was only possible thanks to the technical support of the squadron groundcrew. In wartime, each Wellington squadron had an establishment of around 360 ground personnel. Unlike aircrew, who stayed with a unit for only as long as it took to complete their operational tour of 30 missions, ground personnel remained with the same squadron. Thus, one might define the identity of a squadron by its ground personnel rather than aircrew.

The non-flying side of the squadron was run by the adjutant, and included operational support, administrative and supply staff, as well as the engineering and armament functions. Each squadron was divided into two semi-autonomous flights, which included aircrew and groundcrew. Hangar space might be available for scheduled servicing, but much of the day-to-day maintenance was completed outside at the aircraft dispersal. On most Wellington squadrons a team covering each of the ground trades would be responsible for individual aircraft. 'Fitters' dealt with engines and 'riggers' worked on the airframe itself, while electricians, instrument fitters and wireless mechanics serviced other equipment and systems. Even on well-established stations, accommodation for the maintenance crews was often very crude, and groundcrews worked hard under arduous conditions in the heat of summer and the cold of winter.

If the unit was tasked with operations, the groundcrew carried out the daily inspection and rectified any faults that had been reported by the last crew to have flown the aircraft. Once the aeroplane was declared

Wellington ICs of No 214 Sqn at Stradishall in 1940. The unit eventually received Mk IIs to operate alongside its Mk ICs from November 1941, before both types were replaced by Stirling Is in April 1942 (*BAE Systems courtesy of Brooklands Museum*)

serviceable, aircrew would undertake a Night Flying Test (NFT) to verify the operation of all systems, including the oxygen and intercom systems. Any new or outstanding faults would be fixed on completion of the NFT.

The next job was to prepare the aircraft for operations by filling it with sufficient fuel to reach the target and return to base, and then arming it with the weapon load specified in the operation order. Since the maximum take-off weight would be exceeded with both full fuel tanks and full bomb load, the operational load represented a compromise between these two figures – a long-range target necessitated a smaller weapon load. Bomb loading was also constrained by aircraft centre of gravity limitations. The armourers loaded ordnance into the bomb-bay by means of a hand-cranked winch that was built into the fuselage. They were also responsible for loading ammunition belts for the gun turrets.

When aircrew arrived for their mission, the groundcrew chief assisted the pilot with the engine start. During this procedure another groundcrewman operated the priming pump in the engine nacelle and removed the ground electrical power once the engines were running. Meanwhile, the rest of the groundcrew stood by in case any faults developed requiring last-minute fixing. Then, for the duration of the operation, groundcrew had time to relax, before work started once again when the aircraft returned – if it returned.

During August 1940 No 311 (Czech) Sqn was formed at Honington, with a complement of experienced Czech aircrew. It was commanded by Wg Cdr J F Griffiths, who had previously been a flight commander on No 149 Sqn during the early raids of 1939. The squadron carried out its first operational sortie on the night of 10/11 September, when Sqn Ldr J Schejbal (L7778) and Sgts V Korda (P9235) and F Taiber (L7785) bombed marshalling yards near Brussels. Three aircraft of No 311 Sqn also took part in a major raid on Berlin on the night of 23/24 September, although it lost its first Wellington that night when Plt Off K Trojáček (L7788) suffered an engine failure and force-landed near The Hague. Bomber Command despatched 129 aircraft to attack Berlin, including around 50 Wellingtons from Nos 311, 9, 37, 75, 99 and 149 Sqns. These aircraft bombed a gasworks, a power station, Templehof aerodrome, marshalling yards to the southwest of the city, the Siemens factory and an aero-engine factory. Crews reported heavy, but inaccurate, flak over Berlin and little opposition en route.

The second half of September marked the 'Battle of the Barges', when the strength of Bomber Command was focused on destroying barges gathered in the Channel ports in readiness for an invasion of England. Wellington squadrons were in action against barges in Calais, Boulogne, Ostend, Flushing, Dunkirk and Le Havre every night from 13 to 28 September. The risk of invasion dissipated at the end of the month, so Nos 37 and 38 Sqns were earmarked for service in the Middle East – they deployed to Egypt at the end of October.

This development also coincided with the decision to expand the capability of Bomber Command to carry out long-range bombing raids against Germany by changing the role of No 1 Group and re-equipping its Battle and Blenheim squadrons with more suitable aircraft. Wellingtons, Hampdens or Whitleys were all examined for this role. In the late summer of 1940 there were 221 Wellingtons in storage, with another 62 airframes

stored without engines (the figures for the Hampdens were 58 and 221, respectively), with a factory output of 116 aircraft per month (as against just 40 Hampdens). The reason for the high proportion of airframes stored without engines was a shortage of Pegasus XVIIIs. The few available Whitleys were already considered to be obsolete, so in reality there was only one choice of aircraft type – the Wellington.

The limiting factor in any expansion would prove to be training, since the output of the Wellington OTUs was around 56 crews per month, against a wastage rate (combat and accident losses, plus crews that needed to be withdrawn from the frontline for instructional duties at the OTUs) across all Wellington squadrons of around 51 crews. Furthermore, while the crew of a Battle or Blenheim comprised three men, each Wellington required six aircrew and, of course, the groundcrews would also need to be trained on the new type. The Air Ministry therefore instructed that 12 'medium bomber' squadrons should be amalgamated into six 'heavy bomber' squadrons – the Battle units Nos 12, 142, 103, 150 Sqns, as well as Nos 300 (Polish), 301 (Polish), 304 (Polish) and 305 (Polish) Sqns, plus four former Blenheim units, Nos 15, 40, 57 and 218 Sqn – were to be re-equipped with Wellingtons.

However, the decision was taken at HQ Bomber Command that individual squadron identities should be preserved both for reasons of morale and to allow further expansion to be carried out more easily once crews and aircraft became available. Thus, when the selected units began their conversions to the Wellington in the autumn of 1940, they reformed at half strength. Each unit had a full squadron organization, but two half-flights each of four aircraft.

Bombing operations against Germany continued through October, and Berlin was bombed periodically during the month, on the nights of 7/8 October (by Nos 38, 115, 99, 149 and 214 Sqns), 12/13 October (by Nos 311, 9 and 214 Sqns), 23/24 October (by Nos 37, 75, 99 and 149 Sqns) and 29/30 October (by Nos 99 and 149 Sqns).

German battlecruisers, which had been the focus of Bomber Command operations during the early days of the war, were revisited too. On 16/17 October Nos 99, 149, 38 and 115 Sqns bombed *Gneisenau* and *Scharnhorst*, which were both being repaired in Kiel, and the battleship *Tirpitz*, which was undergoing fitting out in Wilhelmshaven. The following night Nos 37, 75, 214 and 311 Sqns attacked *Gneisenau* and *Scharnhorst* again, as well as *Bismarck*, which was fitting (*text continues on page 45*)

Wellington IC R3175 of No 149 Sqn undergoes engine runs at Mildenhall during the summer of 1940. The aircraft, flown by Plt Off J L Leeds, failed to return from a bombing mission to Boulogne on 9 September that same year *(Philip Jarrett)*

COLOUR PLATES

1
Wellington I L4288/KA-ZA of No 9 Sqn, Honington, 1939

2
Wellington I L4257/LY-P of No 149 Sqn, Mildenhall, 1939

3
Wellington I L4367 of No 75 Sqn, Honington, 1939

4
Wellington I NZ305 of the 'New Zealand Squadron', Marham, 1939

5
Wellington IA P9299/BK-U of No 115 Sqn, Marham, 1939

6
Wellington IA N2871/WS-B of No 9 Sqn, Honington, December 1939

7
Wellington IA N2912/LG-G of No 215 Sqn, Bassingbourn, 1940

8
Wellington IA N2985/AA-M of No 75 Sqn, Harwell, 1940

9
Wellington IA P9273/OJ-N of No 149 Sqn, Mildenhall, 1940

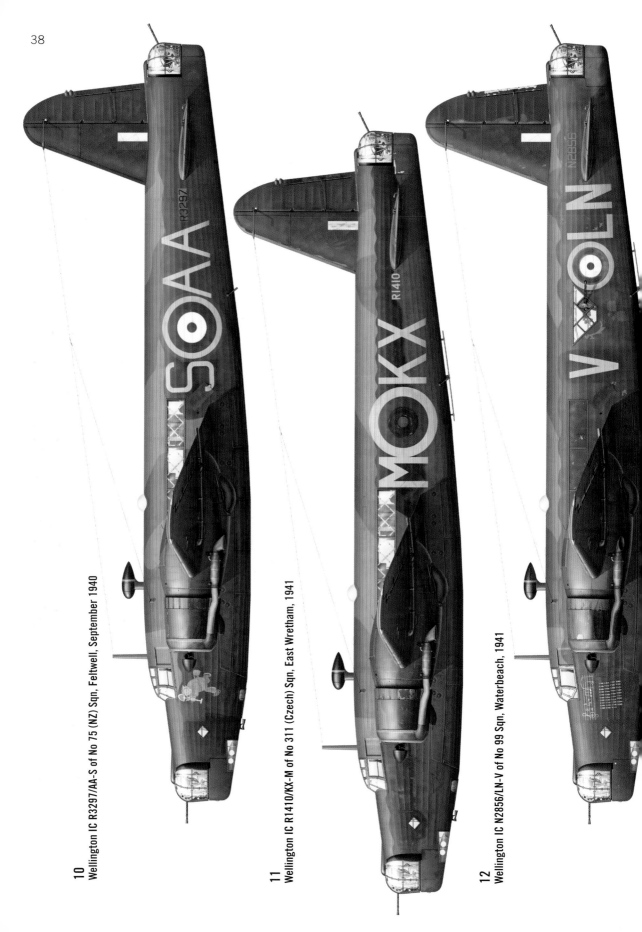

10
Wellington IC R3297/AA-S of No 75 (NZ) Sqn, Feltwell, September 1940

11
Wellington IC R1410/KX-M of No 311 (Czech) Sqn, East Wretham, 1941

12
Wellington IC N2856/LN-V of No 99 Sqn, Waterbeach, 1941

13
Wellington IC W5690/GR-W of No 301 (Polish) Sqn, Hemswell 1941

14
Wellington IC W5612/PM-G of No 103 Sqn, Elsham Wolds, 1941

15
Wellington IC R1697/NZ-S of No 304 (Polish) Sqn, Lindholme, April 1942

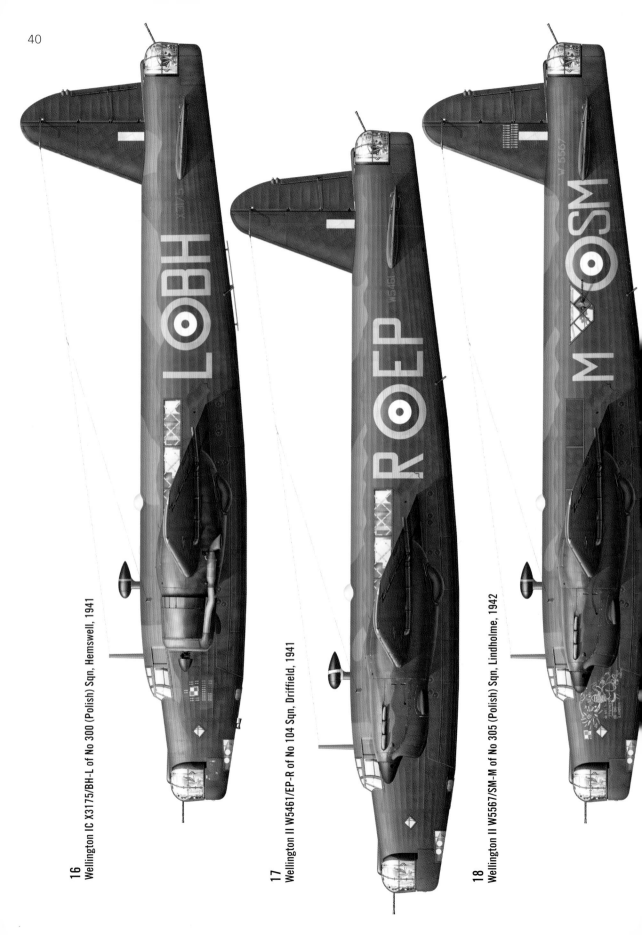

16
Wellington IC X3175/BH-L of No 300 (Polish) Sqn, Hemswell, 1941

17
Wellington II W5461/EP-R of No 104 Sqn, Driffield, 1941

18
Wellington II W5567/SM-M of No 305 (Polish) Sqn, Lindholme, 1942

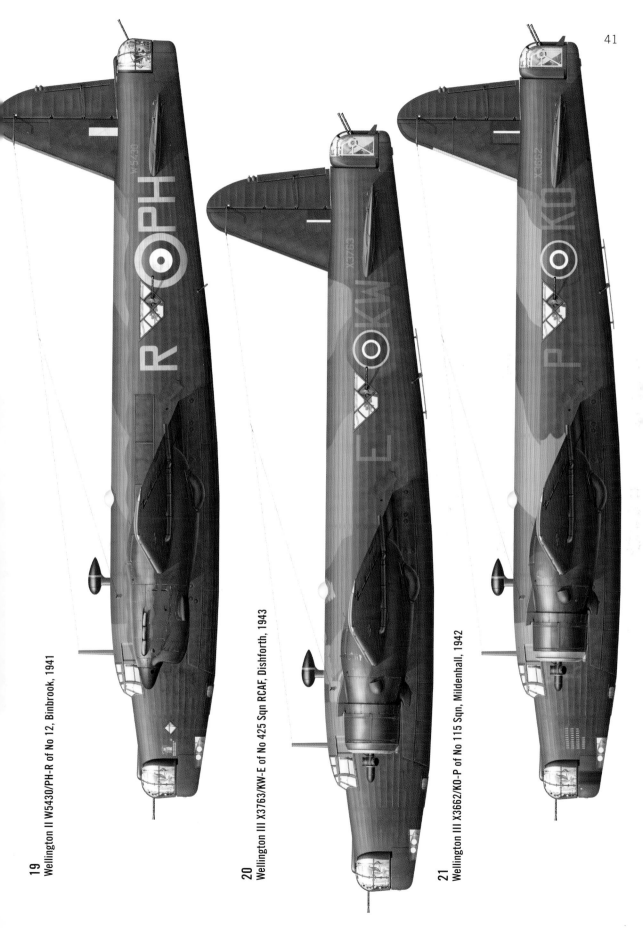

19
Wellington II W5430/PH-R of No 12, Binbrook, 1941

20
Wellington III X3763/KW-E of No 425 Sqn RCAF, Dishforth, 1943

21
Wellington III X3662/KO-P of No 115 Sqn, Mildenhall, 1942

22
Wellington III Z1572/VR-Q of No 419 Sqn RCAF, Mildenhall, May 1942

23
Wellington III BK347/BT-Z of No 30 OTU, Hixon, 1943

24
Wellington IV Z1320/BH-K of No 300 (Polish) Sqn, Hemswell, 1942

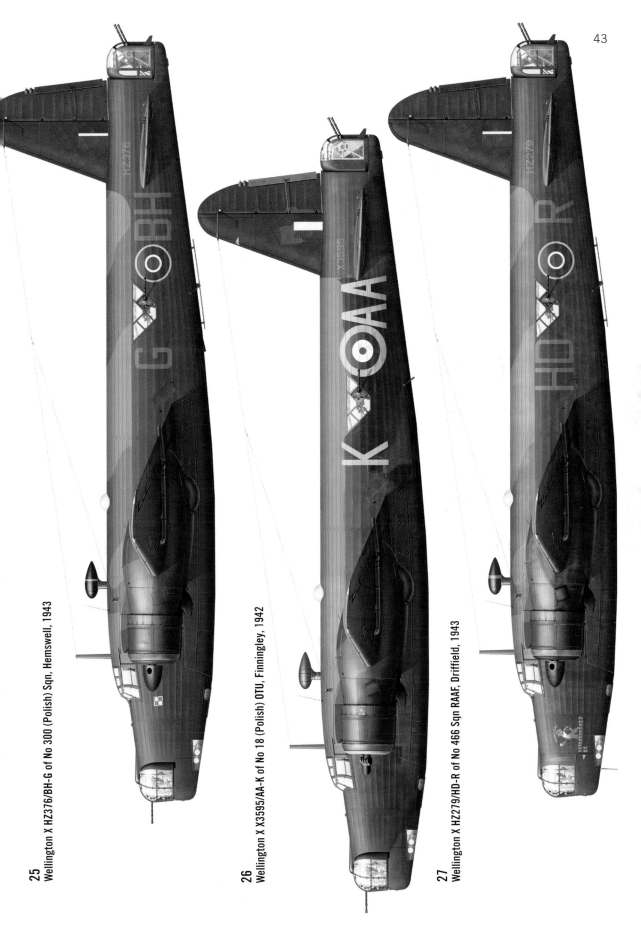

25
Wellington X HZ376/BH-G of No 300 (Polish) Sqn, Hemswell, 1943

26
Wellington X X3595/AA-K of No 18 (Polish) OTU, Finningley, 1942

27
Wellington X HZ279/HD-R of No 466 Sqn RAAF, Driffield, 1943

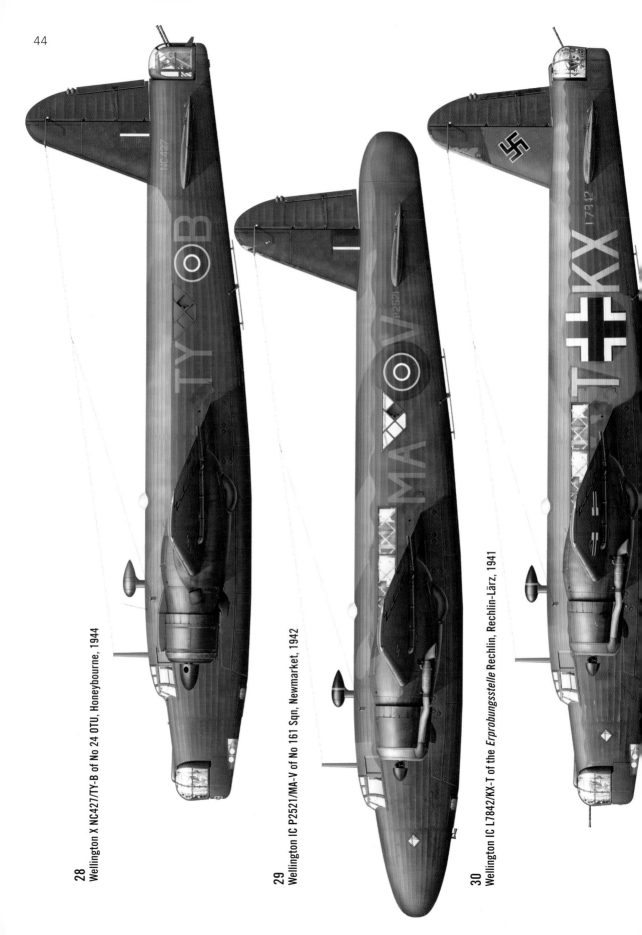

44

28
Wellington X NC427/TY-B of No 24 OTU, Honeybourne, 1944

29
Wellington IC P2521/MA-V of No 161 Sqn, Newmarket, 1942

30
Wellington IC L7842/KX-T of the *Erprobungsstelle* Rechlin, Rechlin-Lärz, 1941

out in Hamburg. Although cloud covered Hamburg, some aircraft made attacks by running in from identifiable landmarks. Heavy flak was reported over Kiel on both nights. On a further raid on 21/22 October, Nos 9, 214 and 37 Sqns attacked *Bismarck* and *Tirpitz* in their respective dockyards.

Bomber Command targeting policy changed towards the end of 1940, favouring a more concentrated application of force rather than piecemeal raids by small numbers of aircraft against disparate targets. The main targets attacked by Wellington squadrons included oil facilities at Emden and Benrath, the Krupps works at Essen, marshalling yards and mining and steel plants at Hamm, chemical and steel works at Duisburg, marshalling yards at Soest and Mannheim and mining, steel and heavy industry at Osnabrück and Gelsenkirchen.

The two new Wellington units based at Binbrook, Nos 12 and 142 Sqns, were equipped with the Vickers Type 406 Wellington II. This variant used the same airframe as the Mk IA, but was powered by Rolls-Royce Merlin X engines. The Merlin was more powerful than the Pegasus XVIII fitted to the Mk IA, so the Mk II enjoyed an improved performance over the earlier models. The Merlin crankshaft also rotated in the opposite sense to the Pegasus, so the Mk II tended to swing to the left on take-off.

Meanwhile, operational experience over the summer had shown the beam gun position introduced in the Wellington IC to be unsatisfactory. A number of different options were investigated before a new mounting was selected, which also included the replacement of the Vickers gas-operated gun by the Browning 0.303-in gun. Writing on 6 November, the Squadron Leader Armaments at No 3 Group described how, in the new arrangement;

'The gun is mounted aft of the under turret opening and can be trained by means of a linkage connected to handles, above which is mounted a deflector sight. The sight is situated close to the side of the fuselage behind an optical panel, and a good field of view is provided by the fitting of Perspex panels. Left- and right-hand mountings are being provided to bring the sights opposite each other so that the gunner can swing quickly round on a species of piano stool from one gun to the other.'

This configuration, which was introduced from December 1940, gave later marks of Wellington the distinctive inverted triangular-shaped windows in the rear fuselage.

Despite a fairly intensive pace of operations, with most squadrons fielding 11 or 12 aircraft for operations, Wellington losses from enemy defences remained relatively low. For example, during October 1940 only nine were lost over Germany – Plt Off D MacLean (R3219) of No 38 Sqn and Sgt L G Goldie (T2549) of No 115 Sqn over Osnabrück on 1 October; Sqn Ldr R O O Taylor (P9287) of No 38 Sqn over Berlin on 7 October; Flg Off R G Furness (P9273) of No 75 (NZ) Sqn and Plt Off W E N Keller (P9243) of No 99 Sqn failed to return from operational sorties on 10 and 13 October, respectively; Sqn Ldr J O Hinks (T2464) of No 9 Sqn was shot down attacking oil installations at Magdeburg on 14 October; Plt Off B Landa (L7844) of No 311 Sqn failed to return on 16 October; and on 24 October Flt Lt E G F Chivers (L7809) of No 38 Sqn and Plt Off R M Sanderson (P9292) of No 75 (NZ) Sqn were downed near Bremerhaven.

In early December, Bomber Command was tasked by the Air Ministry with Operation *Abigail*, which was intended 'as a reprisal for concentrated attacks on places like Coventry and Southampton'. The operational planners envisaged maximum effort from all units, including some crews flying two missions in one night. The objective was to cause widespread uncontrollable fires, which would swamp the civil defences and destroy the city. The bombload was to include High Explosive (HE) ordnance to blow the roofs off buildings and incendiary bombs to start the fires. Various factors, such as size of the settlement, its distance from Britain, the ease of locating the target and also whether or not the civil authorities were practised in dealing with air raids, were considered when producing a short-list of possible targets.

Mannheim was duly selected as the target based on the weather forecasts for mid-December, with the night of 16/17 December being chosen for the attack. Although the city was to have originally been targeted by 200 bombers, in the event, the actual attack was made by only 134 aircraft. This number included 61 Wellingtons drawn from Nos 9, 75 (NZ), 99, 115, 149, 214 and 311 Sqns.

Seven of the 'new' Wellington squadrons mounted their first operations to the Channel ports on consecutive nights in late December. On the 20th No 218 Sqn bombed Ostend and No 15 Sqn attacked Antwerp, and the latter was targeted the following night by five crews from No 40 Sqn while No 150 Sqn bombed Ostend. On the evening of the 22nd Nos 300 (Polish) and 301 (Polish) Sqns made their debut against Antwerp, and No 103 Sqn attacked Ostend.

At the end of 1940, the Order of Battle of frontline Wellington squadrons in Bomber Command was as follows;

No 1 Group

Binbrook	No 12 Sqn (code letters PH)
Newton	No 103 Sqn (PM)
	No 150 Sqn (JN)
Waltham	No 142 Sqn (QT)
Swinderby	No 300 (Polish) Sqn (BH)
	No 301 (Polish) Sqn (GR)
Syerston	No 304 (Polish) Sqn (NZ)
	No 305 (Polish) Sqn (SM)

No 3 Group

Honington	No 9 Sqn (WS)
Wyton	No 15 Sqn (LS)
	No 40 Sqn (BL)
Feltwell	No 57 Sqn (DX)
	No 75 (NZ) Sqn (AA)
Newmarket	No 99 Sqn (LN)
Marham	No 115 Sqn (KO)
	No 218 Sqn (HA)
Mildenhall	No 149 Sqn (OJ)
Stradishall	No 214 Sqn (BU)
East Wretham	No 311 (Czech) Sqn (KX)

The aircrew from an unidentified Polish Wellington squadron gather for a group photograph. The unit would have also been assigned around 360 groundcrew to keep its 16 (and two in-use reserve) aircraft serviceable. Four Wellington units in Bomber Command – Nos 300, 301 304 and 305 Sqns – were manned by Polish personnel (*Wellington Aviation*)

CHAPTER THREE

ON THE OFFENSIVE

In January 1941, 19 Wellington squadrons of Bomber Command accounted for more than half of the 36 units that made up the RAF heavy bomber force. However, these squadrons included some that were not yet combat ready, or were under-strength, or both. Of the five units still in the process of converting to the Wellington, No 57 Sqn completed training in January and flew its first operation on 13 January when Sqn Ldr Foulsham (T1281) led five aircraft against Boulogne.

The remaining units (Nos 12, 142, 304 and 305 Sqns) spent the first months of the year carrying out cross-country flying and practice bombing on the range at Wainfleet, in the Wash. They faced a heavy training burden, with No 12 Sqn, for example, complaining that of six sergeant pilots posted to the unit, all bar one had been trained on single-engined biplanes and all of them were 'untrained for operational flying'. This situation was not helped by the loss of Sqn Ldr P C Lawrence (W5356), an experienced flight commander, in a flying accident at Tollerton on 8 February.

The training task was not confined to the units undergoing conversion to type. With a wastage rate of around three crews per month, frontline squadrons also needed to train the steady throughput of new crews who arrived to replace those lost on operations. Typically, the 'freshmen' crews, as they were called, would carry out their first operation against a relatively 'easy' target such as one of the Channel ports – during most operations, each unit would despatch one or two aircraft against Boulogne, Calais, Ostend, Antwerp or Rotterdam.

The opening months of 1941 saw a continuation of the campaign against oil production and storage and the railway infrastructure. Bremen was visited on the first three nights of the year, followed by other familiar targets in the Ruhr valley such as Gelsenkirchen, Essen and Düsseldorf.

January also saw the start of a long and not entirely successful affiliation between Bomber Command crews and the French port of Brest after the cruiser *Hipper* docked there in late December 1940 at the conclusion of a foray into the Atlantic. On 4 January eight Wellingtons of No 99 Sqn and four from No 15 Sqn launched the first raid against *Hipper*. Exactly a month later, 14 Wellingtons, this time from Nos 99 and 214 Sqns, targeted *Hipper* again, although their efforts were hampered by large red fires emanating black smoke that partially screened the target.

A third raid on 23 February by nine aircraft from No 115 Sqn was not successful – one Wellington returned after take-off and crashed on landing, while three others could not locate the target because of poor weather. Those that made it to Brest were greeted by intense flak, and none of them could pinpoint the exact position of their target. Sgt Brown (R1469) was just off the French coast when his rear gunner, Plt Off Mills, spotted a Bf 110 below and to the left of the Wellington. Brown later reported;

'The rear gunner opened fire with 300 rounds from each gun into the Me 110 pilot's covered cockpit. No fire was returned by the enemy aircraft [E/A]. The E/A was seen to shudder and dip its port wing as it turned to port. Plt Off Mills asked the Captain to turn quickly to the right side, and a stall turn and dive brought his guns to bear again on the enemy's tail unit, which, after 200 rounds from each gun, was seen to lose the port tail fin and rudder. The enemy's nose came up and stalled into a spin, disappearing through the clouds at about 4000 ft.'

Sqn Ldr Van (T2887) suffered flak damage to his hydraulic system and had to make a belly landing at Marham and Sgt E J Milton (R1221) crashed into a tree while attempting to land at Feltwell, killing the entire crew. The following night, 11 Wellingtons from No 99 Sqn, 11 from No 149 Sqn and eight from No 15 Sqn also attempted to bomb *Hipper*. None of these operations caused any damage to the ship, which slipped out of Brest unscathed in mid-March.

In the meantime, other targets attacked by the Wellington force included Turin, Wilhelmshaven, Hamburg, Köln and Bremen (where the Focke-Wulf factory was the main target). The night of 31 March/1 April saw the first use of the 4000-lb High Capacity (HC) bomb, known as the 'Cookie', which was dropped

Armourers load 250-lb GP bombs into the bomb-bay of a No 149 Sqn Wellington IC at Mildenhall. Note the hand-cranked winch mechanism that was built into the fuselage (*Philip Jarrett*)

on Emden by Plt Off Franks (W5439) of No 149 Sqn. At that stage the Wellington II was the only aircraft in Bomber Command capable of carrying a 'Cookie'. Franks reported that he 'dropped 1 x 4,000lb HC bomb from 10,000ft right on target and saw very bright burst and debris flung in the air. Good photo obtained of actual bomb burst. Fire visible for 40 miles'.

By March the Battle of the Atlantic was in full swing, and it seemed that the Germans had the upper hand – Kriegsmarine U-boats were wreaking havoc amongst Allied shipping, *Scharnhorst* and *Gneisenau* were at large in the Atlantic and there was the constant threat that *Bismarck* and *Prinz Eugen* would soon join them. Bomber Command was therefore instructed to abandon the oil campaign and concentrate its resources instead in attacks on German naval targets and shipbuilding industries.

The newly-built U-Boat pens at Lorient were duly bombed on 15 and 21 March by Wellingtons of Nos 15, 214 and 311 (Czech) Sqns. Brest also took on a new significance after 22 March when *Scharnhorst* and *Gneisenau* docked there. The two ships were regularly targeted, starting on the night of 3/4 April when 35 Wellingtons drawn from Nos 40, 57, 115 and 214 Sqns, each armed with seven 500-lb Semi-Armour Piercing (SAP) bombs, attacked them. While returning from this mission Sgt C M Thompson (R1470) of No 115 Sqn was downed by a German nightfighter near Kings Lynn.

The following night it was the turn of 39 Wellingtons from Nos 9, 99, 149 and 311 (Czech) Sqns. There was a third raid on the night of 6/7 April by 47 Wellingtons from Nos 9, 57, 99, 103, 115, 300 (Polish) and 311 (Czech) Sqns, but that was thwarted by cloud cover over the target, causing many of the aircraft to jettison their bombs or bring them home. Kiel was bombed on the following two nights by Wellingtons of Nos 9, 15, 40, 99, 149, 214, 300 (Polish) and 311 (Czech) Sqns, and on the night of 9/10 April it was the turn of Berlin, Bremen and Emden to receive the attention of the Wellington force.

The next night, while No 214 Sqn sent nine aircraft to bomb *Scharnhorst* and *Gneisenau*, No 12 Sqn also flew its first operation – Wg Cdr V Q Blackden (W5375) led four aircraft, each loaded with four 500-lb bombs and two Small Bomb Containers (SBC) of incendiaries, to Emden. Unfortunately, nightfighters were active over the Zuider Zee and Wg Cdr Blackden's aircraft was intercepted and shot down. Sgt Preston (W5422) was more fortunate, being able to return on one engine after being attacked over Texel by a Bf 110 that set fire to the Wellington's port engine.

Four aircraft from No 142 Sqn were tasked to perform the unit's first raid on Boulogne on 15 April, but one Wellington went unserviceable on the ground and another was unable to locate the target and brought its bombs home. Two more units made their operational debut on 25 April during an attack on Rotterdam, No 304 (Polish) Sqn sending a pair of Wellingtons and No 305 (Polish) Sqn three aircraft. A raid on Kiel the previous night had marked the end of No 15 Sqn's brief stint operating the Wellington prior to conversion to the Stirling, and it was not without incident. Sgt A Jones (R1218) ran out of fuel on the return leg and the crew bailed out over Yorkshire.

Newly-delivered Wellington II W5442 of No 214 Sqn is seen at Stradishall in July 1941. The aircraft was subsequently transferred to No 12 Sqn and shot down by a Ju 88C over Holland while returning from a raid against Essen on 9 March 1942 – the bomber had already been hit badly by flak over the target prior to being attacked by the nightfighter. The captain of the aircraft, Plt Off R H Buchanan, and two crew members survived, but the remaining three were killed (*Philip Jarrett*)

During April, two more Wellington units were formed, with No 101 Sqn converting from Blenheims and No 104 Sqn from scratch. While the conversion of existing units from other types was a relatively well-trodden route, the formation of a new squadron presented a number of challenges. Firstly, the aircrew came directly from the training system, and were therefore inexperienced in combat operations. Secondly, not only were the aircrew new to the job, but so too were the groundcrew, who had also only just graduated from technical training and had yet to learn the tricks of the trade in the frontline. Furthermore, space had to be found on new airfields on which accommodation was virtually non-existent.

The new No 104 Sqn, part of No 4 Group, was formed at Driffield, initially as a half squadron with eight aircraft on strength and two more 'in-use reserves'. Eventually it would be expanded to a full squadron establishment of 16 aircraft (plus two in-use reserves). The same technique was used to form No 405 Sqn RCAF, also at Driffield, the following month.

Canadian and Australian squadrons were known as 'Article XV' units, after the clause in the British Commonwealth Air Training Plan (BCATP, but also known in Australia as the Empire Air Training Scheme) that made provision for the formation of distinct operational squadrons under Dominion command. They would be crewed and equipped by the respective Dominion, with ground support provided by the RAF. However, the delay in training Dominion personnel through the BCATP meant that most units were formed with RAF crews. Thus, although No 405 Sqn was nominally an RCAF unit, it was initially manned by RAF personnel until sufficient Canadian crews were trained.

The second half of April saw regular raids by Wellingtons against *Scharnhorst* and *Gneisenau* in Brest, as well as naval targets in Lorient and Kiel and industrial targets in Köln, Hamburg, Mannheim, Emden and Berlin. This pattern continued with the good weather into May, and the Wellington force, now comprising 18 operational squadrons, flew missions on every night during the first fortnight of the month. Typically, half the units in each group would operate on alternate nights, generating somewhere between 55 and 75 Wellington sorties per night. Two or three targets would usually be attacked by the bombers – on 2/3 May the targets were Hamburg and Emden, on 3/4 May Brest and Köln and on 4/5 May Brest and Le Havre. On the night of 5/6 May, however, all 71 Wellingtons on operations bombed Mannheim.

During this first week losses were light, with only Flg Off A Sym (R1443) of No 304 Sqn failing to return from a sortie against Le Havre on 6/7 May, although Sgt D L Nola (R3169) and his crew from No 75 (NZ) Sqn were lost when their aircraft flew into a barrage balloon cable over the Humber and crashed on returning from Hamburg that same night.

The pattern of units operating on alternate nights was broken on 8/9 May when all the Wellington squadrons flew operational missions, putting 109 aircraft over Hamburg and 47 over Bremen. Unfortunately, this increased activity was met with a vigorous defence. Plt Off J R Anderson (R1397) of No 103 Sqn was attacked by a Bf 110 and was lucky to escape, but five other crews were less fortunate. Sqn Ldr F L H Eddison (R1226) and Flt Sgt W H Browell (R3208), both of No 218 Sqn, Sgt C R Burch (R1506) from No 149 Sqn, Flg Off G J Lynes (R1473) of No 304 (Polish) Sqn and Sgt J Dorman (R1322) of No 305 (Polish) Sqn all failed to return.

Thanks to the practice afforded to them by Bomber Command, the German defences were becoming more effective. Many of the 68 Wellingtons that attacked Kiel and the Blohm und Voss works at Hamburg on the night of 10/11 May reported heavy and accurate flak, with searchlight cones adding to defences. Sgt Madgewick (R1511) of No 218 Sqn reported being caught in searchlights at 14,000 ft south of Westerhever on his way to Kiel and escaping by diving to 8000 ft. He was then held again by searchlights in intense flak, so he dived to 50 ft, headed out to sea and bombed Heligoland instead.

That same night Sgt Henderson (W5664) from No 103 Sqn was held in searchlights for 20 minutes at 15,000 ft over Kiel and was unable to locate his target, and squadronmate Plt Off Ball (R1395) was attacked in succession by a Bf 109, two Bf 110s and a Ju 88, noting drily afterwards that 'the crew was unable to recall details owing to the rapidity of the attacks'. The aircraft was badly damaged with the starboard engine partially disabled, so the crew jettisoned all the spare equipment to lighten the bomber. Ball landed at Elsham Wolds with the undercarriage up. Plt Off J W Seivers (R1644) of No 150 Sqn was also attacked four times by a Bf 110 while being held by searchlights, but his gunners shot down the nightfighter. However, despite these close escapes, Sgt J G Keymer (R1512) of No 149 Sqn and Flg Off V C D Spiller (R1435) of No 150 Squn failed to return on that night.

Two of eight Wellingtons from No 311 (Czech) Sqn that participated in the 51-aircraft raid on Hanover on 15/16 May had hair-raising experiences. Flt Sgt J Šnajdr (R1410) was overhead Nienburg when the port engine caught fire. The blaze was successfully extinguished and the crew managed to get as far as the Essex coast on the starboard engine before it cut out due to a lack of fuel and they belly landed at Manningtree, near Colchester. After flak damage caused holes in the fuel tank, Sgt F Fencl (R1466) flew at 200 ft over enemy territory before he, too, ran short of fuel and forced landed at Thurlton, near Great Yarmouth.

One of the six No 103 Sqn crews that took part in this raid suffered a fate that was not uncommon amongst bomber crews.

Plt Off R G Eccles (R1494) experienced a port engine failure and ditched 40 miles off the English coast, but despite having transmitted their position and an extensive search by five aircraft over two days, there was no sign of the wreckage and nothing was ever found of the crew. Sadly, many Bomber Command crews met their fate in this way, having almost made it home, only to be lost at sea before rescuers could find them.

Although Wellington crews were fortunate that the aircraft was fitted with ditching buoyancy tanks, the success of any ditching was affected by a number of factors such as the extent of any battle damage, weather conditions and the state of the sea. If the crew survived the ditching, their continued survival also depended on the aircraft dinghy being undamaged. And of course, any search assumed that the crew had sent a timely SOS message with an accurate position report. With often quite dubious navigational accuracy, there must have been many fruitless searches looking in the wrong places.

The weather over Europe was unsuitable for flying for most of the rest of the month, resulting in many operations being cancelled, although Köln was attacked by Wellingtons on the nights of 16/17, 17/18 and 23/24 May. Poor weather also extended over the Atlantic, hindering the search for *Bismarck* and its heavy cruiser escort *Prinz Eugen*. They had parted company on 25 May and *Bismarck* was sunk two days later. However, the whereabouts of *Prinz Eugen* remained unknown, and on 27 May a strong force of bombers, including 52 Wellingtons from Nos 9, 40, 57, 75 (NZ) and 99 Sqns, flew 8 hr 30 min sorties in an attempt to locate the warship.

The 12 Wellingtons from No 12 Sqn reported that 'a large number of enemy aircraft were encountered and attacks made on our aircraft, but no serious damage was sustained'. However, *Prinz Eugen* evaded detection, and four days later joined *Scharnhorst* and *Gneisenau* at Brest. The latter was bombed on a number of occasions in June, along with Bremen and other regular targets in the Ruhr.

On 9 June, Wg Cdr R G C Arnold (R1758) of No 9 Sqn led four Wellingtons as part of a larger formation of 18 aircraft on a daylight anti-shipping sweep of the English Channel. They were attacked by six Bf 109s four miles northeast of Calais, resulting in the loss of Wg Cdr Arnold and also Flg Off D F Lamb (T2626). The remaining crews, Sqn Ldr Pickard (K5703) and Plt Off Robinson (R1763), escaped by flying into cloud. Three nights later, four Wellingtons of No 405 Sqn RCAF

Wellington IC N2856 of No 99 Sqn, parked in its dispersal at Waterbeach between missions in 1941, has the revised mounting for the beam gun in the new fuselage window just ahead of the roundel. This aircraft was later transferred to No 12 OTU at Benson (*No 99 Sqn Archive*)

performed the unit's first operational mission against the marshalling yards at Schwerte, near Dortmund.

The first Vickers Type 417 Wellington III, powered by 1400 hp Bristol Hercules XI engines, reached No 9 Sqn in June. The most significant development in this version was the improvement of the defensive armament with the introduction of the four-gun Nash & Thompson FN-20A tail turret. Additionally, it was fitted with anti-ice protection, windscreen wipers and balloon cutters. The increased power of the Hercules engines gave the Wellington III a maximum take-off weight of 34,500 lbs, compared to 30,000 lbs for the Mk IC, and although the extra power made no improvement on range or bombload over the latter, it did endow the Mk III with a higher ceiling. Eventually, more than 1500 examples of this version were built, with production evenly divided between Chester and Blackpool. Superseding the Mk IC in operational squadrons, the Wellington III was destined to become the mainstay of Bomber Command through 1941–42.

A raid on Brest on the night of 1/2 July included 46 Wellingtons from Nos 9, 99, 101, 149 and 311 Sqns (plus four more from the latter unit that attacked Cherbourg). Despite an effective smokescreen, the bombers inflicted extensive damage on *Prinz Eugen*. Fourteen aircraft from No 149 Sqn participated in this raid, and two of them (Flg Off S L StV Welch (R1343) and Plt Off J E Horsfield (R1408)) failed to return. Ten Wellingtons from No 218 Sqn that attacked the oil storage tanks at Bremen (out of a total of 53 Wellingtons) the following night included Mk II W5447 (Flt Lt Stokes) armed with a 4000-lb 'Cookie'. The Wellington I variants were unable to carry this weapon, which had been introduced earlier in the year. However, since the Mk II could do so, small numbers of Wellington IIs were issued to units flying the Mk IA/C to give them a heavier bombing capability.

The night of 7/8 July saw a large raid by Bomber Command on Köln, Osnabrück, Münster and Mönchen-Gladbach. Among the ten aircraft from No 75 (NZ) Sqn that attacked Münster was Wellington IC L7818 flown by Canadian Sqn Ldr R P Widdowson. The aircraft was returning from the target at 13,000 ft over the Zuider Zee when it was attacked by a Bf 110 that hit the starboard wing with cannon shells and incendiary bullets, severing a fuel pipe. The rear gunner, Sgt A R J Box, fired back and the fighter was seen diving away with smoke pouring from one engine. However, the wing of the Wellington had caught alight with a fire fed by the broken fuel feed.

After an unsuccessful attempt at putting the blaze out with hand-held fire extinguishers, the crew prepared to abandon the aircraft. At this stage the second pilot, New Zealander Sgt J A Ward, volunteered to climb out of the aircraft and along the wing in an attempt to extinguish the blaze using a canvas engine cover that had been doubling as a cushion in the cockpit. At first Ward was going to discard his parachute in order to reduce the drag force of the slipstream, but navigator Sgt L A Lawton, a fellow New Zealander, persuaded him that he should keep it.

Assisted by Lawton, Ward clambered through the astrodome, attached his parachute and tied himself onto a dinghy rope, which was being paid out by Lawton. By kicking and punching the fabric he was able to fashion

Bombs on trolleys await loading into a Wellington IC of No 301 (Polish) Sqn at Hemswell. The box-like stores are small bomb containers, which were filled with 4-lb incendiary bombs (*BAE Systems courtesy of Brooklands Museum*)

enough foot- and hand-holds to brace himself against the slipstream as he climbed down onto the wing and crawled across to the engine. He smothered the fire and pushed the engine cover into the hole in the wing, but it was blown out again by the force of the slipstream. He managed to repeat this feat for a second time, and although the cover was blown out again and lost into the night air, the immediate danger from the fire had dissipated. Lawton then helped the exhausted Ward back inside the aircraft. Despite extensive damage to the aircraft, including losing much of the fabric over the elevators and tailfin, Widdowson landed back at Feltwell. As a result of his selfless bravery, Sgt Ward was awarded the VC, while Widdowson received the DFC and Box the DFM.

July saw the formation of another Article XV unit, No 458 Sqn RAAF, at Holme-on-Spalding Moor. Once again it was initially raised as a half squadron and manned by RAF crews until sufficient Australians became available. The unit, along with Nos 300 and 301 (Polish) Sqns, was equipped with the Vickers Type 424 Wellington IV. Only 220 examples were built, all of them at Chester. The Mk IV was similar in configuration to the Mk IC, except that it was powered by 1050 hp Pratt & Whitney R-1830 Twin Wasp engines.

The American radials introduced a few challenges. Firstly, the Stromberg injection carburettors were prone to flooding the engine if care was not taken on start-up, and secondly, unlike British engines, there was no automatic boost control system. This meant the engines could be over-boosted by a careless pilot. Like the Merlin engines of the Mk II, the Twin Wasps turned in the opposite direction to the Bristol engines, so unless pilots led slightly with the left throttle, the Mk IV tended to swing to the left on take-off. However, once successfully started, the engines were very reliable, and the Mk IV was the fastest of the Wellington variants.

The raids by Bomber Command through the summer months on *Scharnhorst*, *Gneisenau* and *Prinz Eugen* culminated in a massive daylight attack on 24 July. By then, *Scharnhorst* had moved to La Pallice for sea trials after having been repaired – it was bombed by Halifaxes of Nos 35 and 76 Sqns – although *Gneisenau* and *Prinz Eugen* remained at Brest, and they were the target for a force of 83 Wellingtons. The latter took off from their various bases between 1045 hrs and 1145 hrs and headed for Brest in sections of three.

Amongst the earliest airborne were those from the more northerly stations, including six from No 150 Sqn that departed Snaith, near Goole, in two sections in vic formation. Unfortunately, the rear section returned shortly thereafter when the lead aircraft suffered a failure of the oxygen system. Six bombers from No 103 Sqn, led by Sqn Ldr Lane (R1588), set off from Elsham Wolds and nine aircraft from No 104 Sqn, under the leadership of unit OC Wg Cdr Simonds (W5532), left Driffield. The aircraft were loaded with either one 2000-lb Armour Piercing and four 500-lb SAP bombs or eight of the latter. Further south, nine aircraft left Marham, three from No 115 Sqn led by Sqn Ldr Sindall (W5710) joining up with six from No 218 Sqn led by Sqn Ldr Gibbs (R1008).

For the earlier missions, the weather was fine with good visibility and little cloud, and there was no opposition until the bombers reached the French coast. The first section from No 103 Sqn was attacked by a Bf 109 just before reaching the target area, and Sgt J S Bucknole (N2770), who had dropped back slightly, was shot down. The second section was also attacked by fighters, and over the target all aircraft experienced intense and accurate heavy flak. From the No 104 Sqn formation, Plt Off M S Nicholls (W5438) became detached over the target area and was seen taking evasive action in the midst of an intensive flak barrage, but the aircraft was also reported as being attacked by an enemy fighter. Whatever the reason for its demise, the crew failed to return. All of the other aircraft were damaged by flak, and when Sgt Clark (W5486) found himself detached

Merlin-powered Wellington II W5458 was issued to No 99 Sqn at Newmarket in July 1941. The unit was one of a number of squadrons equipped predominantly with Mk ICs that received a handful of Mk IIs, which gave them the capability to drop 4000-lb 'Cookies' (*No 99 Sqn Archive*)

from his section after dropping his bombs, he managed to join up with a No 218 Sqn formation for protection.

The Marham formation had lost Plt Off M Jolly (R1726) from No 115 Sqn. From the same section, Sgt Chidgey (Z8781) was sure that one of his bombs must have hit *Gneisenau*, as the last weapon in the stick was seen to strike the water just beyond the ship. Leading six aircraft from No 99 Sqn, Wg Cdr Dixon-Wright was also confident of having hit the target – he saw five 500-lb SAP bursts going directly across *Gneisenau*, with two bombs falling on one side of the ship and one on the other, and since he could not see the intervening bursts, he felt certain that one of these must have been a direct hit.

Most Wellingtons attacked from between 12,000 ft and 15,000 ft, although Wg Cdr R H Maw (W5397) led three aircraft from No 12 Sqn in a low-level pass. Unfortunately, the rest of his squadron was not so successful as thunderstorms were beginning to form over the English Channel and they could not find the target. German fighters, too, were taking their toll. Sgt H Heald (W5380) from No 12 Sqn was last seen 70 miles from the English coast flying on one engine, and he failed to return. Three aircraft from No 101 Sqn were attacked off Pointe Saint-Mathieu after they had lost contact with the other Wellingtons. When Flt Lt F H Craig (R1702) was shot down into the sea, Sqn Ldr G R Colenso (R1088) sensibly decided not to continue to the target with just two aircraft and aborted the mission.

After dropping their bombs, most of the formations were engaged by fighters as they left the French coast. Sqn Ldr H Budden (W5583), leading the last of the No 104 Sqn sections, fought off two Bf 109s but was attacked by an unseen fighter over the coast of north Brittany. Both engines cut, the rear turret was hit and the gunner and observer were wounded. The fuselage fabric and bomb-bay doors then caught fire and the aircraft filled with smoke. At this stage, Budden's harness got caught in the controls and the aircraft went into a spin. However, the starboard engine picked up and the pilot managed to regain control at sea level and fly as far as Exeter, where he crash-landed. In recognition of his skill and courage, Budden was awarded an immediate DSO, although he was shot down (in W5461) on 13 August and captured on a mission against Berlin before the decoration could be presented to him.

Flg Off W StC MacNeilly (W5494) was one of six aircraft from No 142 Sqn that were attacked by two Bf 109s as they left the target area. With rear gunner Sgt R S Wallwork killed and other crew members wounded, the damaged aircraft landed at Yeovilton. All seven aircraft from No 57 Sqn survived unscathed, but No 75 (NZ) Sqn lost Sgt D F Streeter (N2854), who failed to return.

From No 40 Sqn, Sgt M Evans RNZAF (T2986) was last seen in a steep dive with the starboard engine on fire, and Plt Off Greer (X9662) also came under attack from a Bf 109, which wounded the rear gunner and killed second pilot Sgt M S Holliday. The fighter made a second attack, closing to 50 yards and wounding the wireless operator, who was manning the beam guns. Luckily the front gunner shot down the enemy aircraft as it positioned for a third pass, by which point the hydraulics had been badly damaged – Plt Off Greer had to fly home with the

Merlin-engined Wellington II W5461 of No 104 Sqn, seen here in the early summer of 1941, was shot down during an operational sortie to Berlin on 13 August that same year while being flown by Sqn Ldr H Budden. He and his crew successfully abandoned the aircraft and were captured (*Philip Jarrett*)

undercarriage and flaps down and the bomb-bay doors open. He landed successfully at St Eval.

The 12 Wellingtons from No 405 Sqn RCAF, led by Wg Cdr P A Gilchrist (W5551), were among the last to drop their bombs, attacking between 1532–1540 hrs from 12,000 ft in the face of intense flak and fighter opposition. Wg Cdr Gilchrist failed to return and Plt Off R V Trueman (W5537) was last seen diving steeply pursued by a Bf 109. Sgt N T K Scott (L5530/L) was certain that he had achieved a direct hit on *Gneisenau* prior to being attacked by a Bf 109 over Brest and his aircraft badly damaged. The Wellington crash-landed at Plymouth, where the rear gunner, Sgt H Dearnley, died of wounds he had received during the engagement. Sgt J W Craig (W5581) was also attacked by four Bf 109s. His gunners claimed to have shot down two of them, although enemy shells set the fuselage alight and the rear turret was put out of action. The aircraft could not maintain height and it gradually descended to the sea, crashing 300 yards off the English coast – the crew was rescued. Despite the courageous efforts and optimistic claims of Bomber Command's Wellington crews, *Gneisenau* was not hit during the attacks.

Night operations during August were punctuated by periods of poor weather, with Wellington units only seeing action whenever conditions permitted. Targets included Karlsruhe, Aachen, Hamm, Essen and Duisburg. On 14 August, 12 Wellingtons from No 12 Sqn attacked Magdeburg, where they encountered heavy flak. While manoeuvring aggressively to avoid the defences, Sgt M S Duder (W5578) lost control over the target and rear gunner Sgt J Kyle bailed out as the aircraft plummeted earthwards. Kyle was killed, but Duder managed to regain control and fly home, successfully force landing at Martlesham Heath. From the same unit, Sgt A. Cameron (W5536) was attacked by a Ju 88 while returning from Rotterdam and he crashed near Grimsby.

During the first fortnight of August, D M Bensusan-Butt, working in the Admiralty Statistical Section, analysed the accuracy of the Bomber Command campaign against Germany based on photographic evidence of the raids flown in June and July. His report, published on 18 August, made uncomfortable reading. According to his analysis, on average only one third of the aircraft that claimed to have made successful attacks actually got within five miles of their targets. The figure was nearer ten per cent for attacks on targets in the Ruhr area, but, conversely, almost two-thirds of aircraft attacking the French ports such as Brest were successful in reaching the correct dropping point. Although there was no doubting the courage or tenacity of Bomber Command crews, the report did serve to highlight that the night bombing campaign against Germany was compromised by inadequate equipment and poor training.

The accuracy of bombing attacks cannot have been helped by raids such as the one on Essen on 31 August, where most of the ten aircraft from No 12 Sqn dropped over complete cloud cover.

Brest was bombed again on the night of 3/4 September, and target identification was hampered by poor weather and a defensive smoke screen. Nevertheless, Sgt Youseman in No 99 Sqn Wellington II W5458 delivered a 4000-lb 'Cookie' onto the docks on the eastern bank of the river. The same squadron sortied three of its Mk IIs four nights later to deliver more 4000-lb bombs to Berlin. The force on this raid also included ten Wellingtons from No 12 Sqn, which lost flight commanders Sqn Ldrs S S Fielden (Z8328) and P F Edinger (W5598).

Another loss occurred on 15 September when 12 Wellingtons from No 75 (NZ) Sqn were amongst the force attacking Hamburg. The weather was clear over the target and the defences were well coordinated, with searchlights working in cones and cooperating with both flak batteries and nightfighters. Two of the squadron's aircraft failed to return, one of which (X3205) was flown by VC recipient Sgt Ward on his 11th operational mission. The aircraft was hit repeatedly by flak over the target and it caught fire. Two crew bailed out successfully, but the remaining four, including Ward, were killed.

Later in the month, the reach of the bomber force was extended with missions against Szczecin (Stettin) and Genoa. Three missions, each of about 50 Wellingtons, were mounted against Szczecin on the nights of 19/20, 29/30 September and 30 September/1 October. Returning from the first raid, Plt Off I C Burke (W5384) of No 142 Sqn suffered starboard engine failure and he ditched eight miles off Orfordness, but only rear gunner Sgt T W Rayment survived. Although the weather

Wellington ICs of No 57 Sqn are prepared for their next mission from Feltwell in the summer of 1941. The Norfolk bomber base was home to the unit throughout its association with the Wellington, which commenced in November 1940 when Mk IA/Cs replaced Blenheim IVs, and ended in September 1942 when No 57 Sqn moved to Scampton to convert to the Lancaster I. Wellington detachments from the unit also routinely used Feltwell's dispersal airfield at nearby Methwold (*Graham Pitchfork*)

was good and there was clear moonlight (particularly on the third raid), all crews reported that the bombing was scattered.

The weather was not so good for the first raid against Genoa on the night of 26/27 September, and a general recall was transmitted to 34 Wellingtons from Nos 9, 57, 99, 149 and 311 Sqns participating in the mission. The recall also extended to 16 Wellingtons targeting the railway station in Köln and six sent to Emden. One of the No 115 Sqn 'freshmen', Sgt J Horabin (R1332), sent out an SOS signal reporting that he had an engine fire, and he failed to return from the mission to Emden. Four Wellingtons from No 311 (Czech) Sqn had set out for Genoa, and Sgt Musálek (T2553) did not receive the recall message and continued on alone to northern Italy. He found Genoa to be under total cloud cover, so he dropped his bombs over the estimated target position from 14,000 ft in the middle of a barrage of light tracer flak. A second raid on Genoa, carried out two nights later by 41 Wellingtons from the same squadrons (as well as a further 17 operating against Frankfurt and Emden), was more successful.

Nürnberg was the target of two raids in mid-October. A force of 108 Wellingtons sortied on the night of 12/13 October against Nürnberg and Bremen, losing two aircraft over Nürnberg and one over Bremen. In a vindication of Bensusan-Butt's findings, many bombs dropped on this raid were reported by German authorities to have landed between Stuttgart and Lauingen, nearly 100 miles away from Nürnberg. Two nights later, the same targets were attacked, with a similar attrition rate. All three aircraft lost over Nürnberg that night were from No 40 Sqn – Sgt K G Edis (Z8782), Plt Off G B Buse (X9926) and Sgt J R Hiscock (X9882).

By the autumn of 1941, the strategic situation had stabilized. The opening of the Eastern Front by the Germans that summer ensured that Britain was no longer in danger of invasion, the tide was beginning to turn in the Battle of the Atlantic and in North Africa the Afrika Korps was held near the Libyan border. Although Bomber Command was still expanding and building its strength, the decision was taken to deploy two squadrons to the Middle East. On 15 October, 15 Wellingtons from No 104 Sqn, led by Wg Cdr P R Beare, set off from Driffield bound for Malta. They were followed by No 40 Sqn, which was formally stood down from Bomber Command operations on 17 October. Both units left rear elements based in Britain that continued to fly a modest number of aircraft on operations over Germany through the winter.

Meanwhile, the bomber offensive was gaining momentum, with Bomber Command now able to mount large-scale attacks on targets in enemy territory. In December 1940, 200 bombers had been considered a sizeable force, but by November of the following year the expansion of the Command allowed much larger numbers to be fielded. On the night of 7/8 November a force of nearly 400 bombers included 160 Wellingtons alone, drawn from all 19 squadrons, as well as Hampdens, Whitleys, Stirlings, Avro Manchesters and Halifaxes from other units across Bomber Command. The main targets for the Wellingtons that night were Berlin and Mannheim, while a handful of 'freshmen' attacked Boulogne and Ostend. The aircraft carried mixed loads of 1000-, 500- and 250-lb bombs, plus SBCs filled with incendiaries.

Those targeting Berlin encountered thick cloud, forcing the five Wellingtons of No 12 Sqn to climb high in an attempt to avoid them. Six aircraft from No 9 Sqn and 11 from No 218 Sqn also found their targets obscured by cloud once they too reached Berlin. However, conditions over Mannheim were better thanks to an almost full moon and good visibility. Unfortunately, the wind had changed in both direction and strength during the evening and No 150 Sqn reported that some of its Wellingtons were as much as 90 minutes late in reaching the target. Once there, they were greeted by accurate flak and well-coordinated nightfighters.

The German defences were particularly effective that night, with the losses amongst the bomber force amounting to nearly 40 aircraft. This represented a loss rate of ten per cent, which was unsustainable. Those losses included 17 Wellingtons – Sgts S D C Gray (T8903) and A H T Cook (Z8985) from No 57 Sqn, Plt Off W R Methven (X9951) and Flt Sgt J W Black (X9976) from No 75 (NZ) Sqn, Plt Offs C G Gilmore (T2516) and Moore (X9739) and Flt Lt J P Dickinson (T2554) from No 99 Sqn, Plt Off W D C Hardie (R1701) from No 101 Sqn, Plt Off E V Lawson (X9794) from No 103 Sqn, Sgt S A Hart (Z1211) from No 142 Sqn, Sgt S W Dane (X9878) from No 149 Sqn, Sgt L J Atkins (R1606) from No 150 Sqn, Sgt J R C McGlashan (Z1069) from No 218 Sqn, Sgts P Nowakowski (Z1271) and K Sobczak (R1705) from No 300 (Polish) Sqn, Flg Off T Blicharz (R1215) from No 304 (Polish) Sqn and Sgt A L D Hassan (W5555) from No 405 Sqn RCAF.

During November, the composition of the Wellington force changed slightly when No 149 Sqn converted to Stirlings. Its place was taken by No 460 Squadron RAAF, which formed at Molesworth on 15 November. The new unit, which operated Wellington IVs, came under the command of the newly-formed No 8 Group. In order to make the formation of the new Article XV squadron as efficient as possible, it was expanded from 'C' Flight of No 458 Sqn RAAF so that the unit would start off with a nucleus of experienced air- and groundcrew. Canadian unit No 419 Sqn RCAF was also formed at Mildenhall on 15 December.

Bombing operations continued through the last weeks of the year, albeit at a reduced rate while the Air Ministry pondered the lessons to be drawn from the Berlin/Mannheim raid. Targets for the Wellington squadrons

No 300 (Polish) Sqn Wellington IC R1347, flown by Sgt Wielondek, returned to Hemswell with what appears to be flak damage to its left wing and rear fuselage following an attack on Hamburg on 9 August 1941 (*BAE Systems courtesy of Brooklands Museum*)

during this period included Aachen, Düsseldorf, Bremen, Wilhelmshaven and Brest. The final raid of 1941 was mounted by a force including 94 Wellingtons on the night of 28/29 December against Wilhelmshaven and Emden. Weather conditions were perfect, with bright moonlight preceding a heavy frost, but it was a cold night and two Wellingtons from No 218 Sqn had their gun turrets freeze up. The reception over the target, however, was a warm one from an intense barrage of both heavy and light flak guns. Sgt E J Williams (W5561) of No 405 Sqn RCAF and Sgt A Šiška (T2553) from No 311 (Czech) Sqn were lost.

After his Wellington was seriously damaged by flak over Wilhelmshaven, Šiška was forced to ditch midway across the North Sea. Five crew survived the ditching and managed to get into the dinghy. For six bitterly cold winter nights they were left to the mercy of the North Sea. Miraculously, the dinghy was washed up on the northwestern shore of the Netherlands to the south of Den Helder on 3 January 1942, but by then only Šiška, Flg Off J Ščerba (wireless operator) and Sgt P Svoboda (front gunner) were still alive. All three men were taken prisoner and survived the war.

At the end of December 1941, the Air Order of Battle of operational Wellington squadrons within Bomber Command was as follows;

No 1 Group

Binbrook	No 12 Sqn (PH)
Elsham Wolds	No 103 Sqn (PM)
Grimsby	No 142 Sqn (QT)
Snaith	No 150 Sqn (JN)
Hemswell	No 300 (Polish) Sqn (BH)
	No 301 (Polish) Sqn (GR)
Lindholme	No 304 (Polish) Sqn (NZ)
	No 305 (Polish) Sqn (SM)
Holme-on-Spalding Moor	No 458 Sqn RAAF (MD)

No 3 Group

Honington	No 9 Sqn (WS)
Alconbury	No 40 Sqn (part) (BL)
Feltwell	No 57 Sqn (DX)
	No 75 (NZ) Sqn (AA)
Marham	No 115 Sqn (KO)
	No 218 Sqn (HA)
Waterbeach	No 99 Sqn (LN)
Oakington	No 101 Sqn (SR)
Stradishall	No 214 Sqn (UX)
East Wretham	No 311 (Czech) Sqn (KX)
Mildenhall	No 419 Sqn RCAF (VR)

No 4 Group

Driffield	No 104 Sqn (part) (EP)
Pocklington	No 405 Sqn RCAF (LQ)

No 8 Group

Molesworth	No 460 Sqn RAAF (UV)

CHAPTER FOUR

PEAK STRENGTH

For the first few weeks of 1942, the focus of Bomber Command was very firmly on Brest. *Scharnhorst*, *Gneisenau* and *Prinz Eugen* were all seaworthy once more, and it was only a matter of time before they attempted to break out into the open sea. Brest was attacked by Wellingtons on almost every night for the first half of January, including raids by No 99 Sqn on 8 January and by newly-formed No 419 Sqn RCAF on 11 January. The raid by No 99 Sqn was one of its last missions over Europe before deployment to the Far East, while that by No 419 Sqn RCAF was the first operation by the Canadian unit, and comprised just two crews, Wg Cdr Fulton (X9748) and Plt Off Cottier (Z1145).

From mid-January, attacks concentrated on the Ruhr, but Brest was revisited on 26/27 January by a force including Wellingtons from Nos 103 and 214 Sqns. Although Bomber Command had gained No 419 Sqn RCAF at Mildenhall during the month, the number of Wellington units remained constant during January as No 218 Sqn converted to Stirlings.

Brest was targeted a number of times in early February, and on the night of 11/12 February seven Wellingtons from No 103 Sqn bombed the port. The weather was foul so none of the crews, who bombed over a solid cloud base, could have known that the warships had already slipped out of port and were preparing to sail up the English Channel. In fact, their progress was not detected until nearly midday, when the call went out for all available aircraft to mount operations against them.

A Wellington III of No 419 Sqn RCAF. This 'Article XV' unit was formed at Mildenhall on 15 December 1941 and flew its first operational mission in January 1942 (*Philip Jarrett*)

The first Wellingtons to get airborne were nine aircraft from No 50 Sqn, which had been held at two hours' standby since 0800 hrs. They took off in three sections at 1330 hrs, led by Wg Cdr Mellor (X9814), just 45 minutes after receiving the order. The German convoy was reported as being between Dover and Calais and the Wellingtons climbed to 8000 ft, with total cloud cover beneath them. On reaching the estimated target position, they descended to 3000 ft and spent the next two hours combing the area in low visibility without result. However, four Wellingtons from No 142 Sqn which left Grimsby at 1340 hrs did find the ships and attacked them from low-level on a northwesterly heading. Flt Sgt W F Caldow (Z1338) reported '1515 hrs, 300 ft, 200 mph IAS, bombs dropped. Course 340, visibility good 7/10 cloud at 1200 ft. Eight or nine ME 109 seen in line circling enemy ships at 1000 yds on port beam. Two enemy aircraft approached to 200 yds slightly above in line astern, one enemy aircraft broke away without firing, the other fired machine gun from nose at 400 yds and Wellington rear gunner replied with two long bursts. Enemy aircraft broke away at 250 yds and tracer from Wellington appeared to enter underside of fuselage. Wellington was not hit'.

Despite extensive searching, eight Wellingtons from No 301 (Polish) Sqn and four from Nos 300 (Polish) and 101 Sqns could not find the German warships. Of the ten Wellingtons from No 214 Sqn that took off at 1500 hrs, Wg Cdr R D B MacFadden (Z1981) was seen by another Wellington circling, with occasional puffs of black smoke coming out of the port engine. Z1981 failed to return from the sortie. Most of the remainder of MacFadden's formation drew a blank in their searching, but Plt Off F J Ruoff (Z1158) descended to 300 ft at 1730 hrs and saw the wake of a large ship. As he turned to follow it, getting ready to attack, the Wellington was intercepted by a Bf 110, into which the rear gunner, Sgt Williams, fired three bursts. However, in evading the attacker the Wellington climbed back into cloud, so Ruoff brought his bombs home.

Although two of five Wellingtons from No 103 Sqn also located the ships, the 300-ft cloud base was too low for Flt Lt D. W. Holford (Z8843) and Flt Sgt Kitney (T2921) to make a successful attack with the SAP bombs loaded on their aircraft. Sqn Ldr I. K. P. Cross (Z8714) failed to return from this sortie.

From No 57 Sqn, Sgt Heald (Z1568), one of four aircraft launched by the unit, bombed one battlecruiser accompanied by three destroyers at 1705 hrs. He dropped seven 500-lb bombs, but was 'unable to state whether hits obtained owing to evasive action'. Seven more Wellingtons from No 12 Sqn, each loaded with eight 500-lb GP bombs, were led by Wg Cdr A Golding. Plt Off N W Richardson (Z8342) located the target ships under an 800 ft cloud base, but with visibility less than 1000 yards. He subsequently reported that 'at first attempt to attack, aircraft hit by light calibre shells; 3 ft hole knocked in starboard tailplane, another shell passed harmlessly through the fuselage just aft of the astrodome and did not explode. The third shell burst inside the cockpit, riddling same; the Captain sustained wound in upper arm. Five minutes later, after stalking in cloud, Captain attacked in shallow dive and bombs released at 400 ft, pulled out of dive at 10 ft, losing trailing aerial. Bombs seen to explode in short stick 15 yds ahead of *Prinz Eugen*. Captain remained at controls until aircraft landed at base 1hr 30mins later. During dive, front gunner raked vessel's deck'. From the same squadron, Plt Off J M Garlick also attacked 'large vessel escorted by six destroyers'.

Taking off from Lakenheath at 1450 hrs, Plt Off Runagall (Z1084) and Sgt Reynolds (X9875) from No 115 Sqn were tasked with attacking flak vessels escorting the capital ships. They were unable to locate the target because of the cloud, although conditions had improved slightly for Sgt Slade (X9831), who took off nearly two hours later. He dropped his bombs from 2000 ft, noticing that they fell some distance ahead of the ships. Two aircraft from No 75 (NZ) Sqn could not find the ships because of cloud, but Plt Off Climie (X3390) was fired on by flak and attacked by two Bf 110s, although no damage was sustained.

Two of the three aircraft from No 419 Sqn RCAF that took off at 1700 hrs failed to return. Six Wellingtons were launched by No 405 Sqn RCAF shortly thereafter, and at 1809 hrs a momentary cloud break gave Sgt Wigley (Z8412) and Plt Off Thiele (Z8428) a fleeting glimpse of the German vessels. 'Although both captains clearly identified one of the big ships, bombing results could not be observed since the target was screened from view immediately following release of the bombs'. Sgt Wigley had dropped his bombs from 3500 ft, but having not had time to attack, Plt Off Thiele searched again for 30 minutes but could not relocate his quarry. 'Both captains say that they were violently engaged by the warships, and noted reduced speed of the ships owing to the lack of wake and no high water at the bows'. All three vessels reached German ports safely that evening, although *Scharnhorst* had been damaged by a mine.

When Nos 40 and 104 Sqns had deployed to the Middle East in late 1941, both units had left behind rear echelons. These were used as cadres from which to form two more Wellington squadrons during February. At Alconbury, the rump of No 40 Sqn became No 156 Sqn, while the rear party of No 104 Sqn at Driffield became No 158 Sqn. The first operation by No 156 Sqn was a 'Nickelling' sortie by Sqn Ldr McGillivray (Z8969) on the night of 16/17 February, and four aircraft flew bombing sorties the next night.

On the night of 3/4 March the Renault factory at Billancourt, near Paris, was the target for 235 bombers. The largest raid by Bomber Command to date, a total of 89 Wellingtons participated in the mission, including 11 from No 12 Sqn, whose crews reported 'no defences at all at Paris – congestion over the target made risk of collision the only danger'. Similarly, No 214 Sqn, which despatched eight Wellingtons, noted that the 'Renault works on the island and on the east bank of the Seine were clearly identified'. However, bomber crews were not often treated to relatively short-range attacks over defenceless parts of France.

Wearing a Sidcot pattern flying suit, and with a belt of 0.303-in ammunition over his right arm, a gunner heads aft towards the rear turret. The circular frame beneath the catwalk was the aperture used for the long since abandoned 'dustbin' ventral turret fitted in the Wellington IA (*State Library Victoria*)

Indeed, a campaign against Essen, in the industrial heartland of the Ruhr, started on the night of 8/9 March, with subsequent raids on the nights of 9/10, 10/11, 25/26 and 26/27 March. This marked a new tactic by Bomber Command of mounting large raids against the same target on two or three consecutive nights. Meanwhile, the introduction of the TR1335 Gee radio-navigation system in early 1942 helped to improve navigation, and also gave a limited capability for aircraft to 'blind bomb' over cloud cover. In another new tactic, known as 'Shaker', Gee-equipped aircraft helped the main force locate the target. 'Shaker' was pioneered by No 101 Sqn Wellingtons during the raid on Essen on 8/9 March, some of the aircraft being loaded with 4.5-inch parachute flares to illuminate the target, while others were armed exclusively with incendiary bombs intended to mark the target from the ground by starting large-scale fires.

Amongst the five Wellington losses over Essen on 8/9 March was Sgt M S Duder (Z8409) of No 12 Sqn, who had had the lucky escape over Magdeburg the previous August. Ten Wellingtons were lost on the raid on 26/27 March, including OC No 12 Sqn, Wg Cdr A Golding (W5372). A post-raid report by the unit's Plt Off J M Garlick (Z1612/Z) gives an idea of the challenges facing crews as defences became more efficient;

'Our aircraft was held in a cone of searchlights, and in spite of evasive action, was passed to further cones. IFF was used but without apparent effect. Rear gunner observed one twin-engined aircraft, believed to be a Ju 88, approximately 200 yards astern and proceeded to shadow our aircraft for approximately five minutes, during which time the enemy aircraft delivered at least five attacks from astern and both quarters, although our aircraft, after the believed identification, was unable to make further observation other than momentary ones from enemy aircraft tracks of tracer owing to searchlight glare. Our aircraft took diving turn to port and violent evasive action down to 700–800 ft after which no further attacks were made by enemy aircraft and presumably lost sight of our aircraft which was by then out of searchlights. Our rear gunner fired short burst on first observing enemy aircraft and at least a further nine short bursts at presumed position of enemy aircraft, all with unobserved results. Our aircraft was holed by machine gun fire slightly in front of rear turret but not affecting efficiency of aircraft. The crew sustained no casualties.'

Other targets attacked during the month included Köln on 13/14 March, with a number of Wellingtons using their Gee equipment and bombs 'released on TR [1335] fix'. Saint-Nazaire and Lübeck were also attacked, and on 12/13 March No 460 Sqn RAAF flew its first operational mission when four aircraft bombed Emden. March also saw the departure of No 458 Sqn RAAF for the Middle East.

An innovative tactic was trialled, perhaps appropriately, on 1/2 April during a low-level attack on the marshalling yards at Hanau Lohr, near Frankfurt. Thirty-five Wellingtons, drawn from Nos 57, 75 (NZ) and 214 Sqns, joined 14 Hampdens for the mission. Unfortunately, the raid was disastrous – No 57 Sqn lost five of its 11 aircraft and No 214 Sqn lost seven of 12 Wellingtons. Plt Off Shepherd (Z1566) of No 75 (NZ) Sqn had a very lucky escape, having been chased by nightfighters for 30 miles from Brussels, but he managed to evade them.

Over the next few nights Köln and Essen were re-visited in force, and on 8/9 April the largest raid by Bomber Command to date was mounted against Hamburg. Of a total force of 272 bombers, 177 were Wellingtons. No 101 Sqn was given the job of marking the target with incendiaries.

The following day, seven Wellingtons set out on daylight 'cloud cover' raids against Essen. This was not the first such mission (it was initially tried on 4 April), and the raids were designed to be a nuisance to the German defences. Crews were tasked with getting as far as they could using cloud cover for their own protection. Taking off at 1230hrs, Sqn Ldr G F Phipps (Z1564) led four Wellingtons from No 57 Sqn, but the sortie was abandoned over enemy territory because of a lack of cloud cover. Three more Wellingtons from No 75 (NZ) Sqn also participated, and although two returned to base because of insufficient cloud cover, Plt Off Fisher (X3720) continued into Germany and dropped his bombs near Geldern, west of Duisburg. No enemy aircraft were seen during the sortie, and Fisher encountered only isolated bursts of flak.

Essen was also attacked on the nights of 10/11 and 12/13 April, after which Bomber Command concentrated on Dortmund for two nights and, on 17/18 April turned its attention to Hamburg once more. Crews from eight Wellingtons despatched by No 75 (NZ) Sqn reported intense, heavy, flak, cooperating with numerous searchlights, and seven bombers were lost on this raid. The casualties included Sqn Ldr Phipps of No 57 Sqn, who had led the cloud cover raid only days previously. Two raids against Köln on 22/23 and 27/28 April were interspersed with three nights of attacks against the Heinkel factory at Rostock. Once again, seven No 101 Sqn crews marked the target with incendiaries, and three crews from No 142 Sqn who attacked Rostock experienced only slight defences, with large fires visible for 100 miles.

The number of Wellington squadrons in Bomber Command reduced slightly over the next two months with the transfer to Coastal Command of No 311 (Czech) Sqn in April and No 304 (Polish) Sqn in May. Two more units converted to four-engined types in April, No 214 Sqn re-equipping with the Stirling and No 405 Sqn RCAF receiving the Halifax – Nos 103 and 158 Sqns also converted to the Halifax in June.

Wellington IC R1697 of No 304 (Polish) Sqn force landed at Lindholme after being severely damaged by a Bf 110 over Flensburg while returning from bombing Rostock on 25 April 1942 (*Wojtek Matusiak*)

Two 1500-lb sea mines are readied for loading into a Wellington III. Bomber Command carried out an extensive mine dropping campaign throughout 1942–43, in which the Wellington squadrons played a major role (*Wellington Aviation*)

In early 1942 the role of second pilot was discontinued since all of the four-engined aircraft operated by Bomber Command had only one pilot. The roles of navigator and bomb aimer had also been separated, so, from mid-1942, most Wellingtons were flown by a crew of five comprising pilot, navigator, bomb aimer, wireless operator/air gunner and rear gunner.

Stuttgart was bombed on the nights of 4/5, 5/6 and 6/7 May, and five Wellingtons failed to return from the third raid. However, the main role played by Bomber Command Wellingtons during the month was that of mine laying. These sorties were code-named 'gardening', and for much of the summer Wellington units carried out such sorties each night. The whole of the northern European coast from the Bay of Biscay to the Baltic was divided into areas, or 'gardens', each named after a plant or fruit, and bombers were despatched to sow mines in the various areas. However, the main focus was on the French U-boat ports in the Bay of Biscay, the shipping lanes used by coastal convoys amongst the Frisian Islands and also the Baltic coast.

A Wellington could carry one or two 1500-lb parachute mines (known as 'vegetables'). These were dropped from relatively low level, below 1500 ft, which exposed crews to the risks involved in low flying at night, often in poor weather, and opposed by coastal flak batteries. 'Gardening' sorties were perceived as being relatively easy, low threat missions, but losses did nevertheless occur on these operations. Two Wellingtons failed to return from mine laying over the Baltic on the night of 15/16 May and two more were lost two nights later, again over the Baltic.

Cloud cover raids also continued through the summer. On 13 May Sgt Evans (X3387) was the first of three Wellingtons from No 57 Sqn to attack Essen/Mulheim individually. One aircraft was recalled, but two others pressed on and dropped their weapons successfully.

The new Air Officer Commanding-in-Chief (AOC-in-C) Bomber Command, Air Marshal Sir A T Harris, was determined to increase the momentum of the bomber campaign against Germany and planned to put 1000 aircraft over a single target on a single night. At the time the most that Bomber Command had managed on any night was less than 300, so a massive effort would be needed to carry out the 'thousand plan', which had been code-named Operation *Millennium*. Each squadron readied the maximum number of aircraft for operations, and the OTUs were also tasked with providing as many bombers as possible.

Although there was heavy rain in England, the weather conditions over Germany were ideal on the night of 30/31 May, and a total of 1047 bombers participated in an attack on Köln. The majority of them were

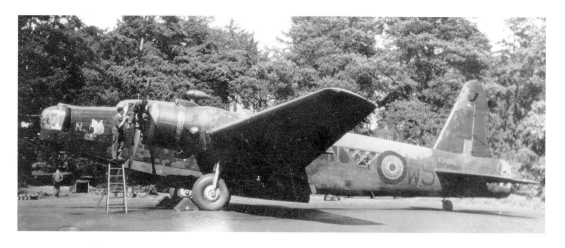

Wellingtons, with more than 600 targeting Köln that night, and 228 of the bombers were from the OTUs. Many of the Wellington squadrons launched impressive numbers of aircraft – No 12 Sqn sent 28 Wellingtons, the largest number ever sortied by the squadron, No 75 (NZ) Sqn fielded 23 aircraft, No 142 Sqn 22 aircraft and No 57 Sqn 20 aircraft. The bomber stream routed via Cromer and Dunkirk to the target and returned by way of Vlissingen and Aldeburgh.

Wellington III X3666 of No 9 Sqn was flown by Canadian Sgt Vic 'Trusty' Trustrum on the night of 30/31 May 1942 during the Operation *Millennium* attack on Köln (*RAF Museum*)

The operations diary for No 103 Sqn, which sent 19 Wellingtons, recorded that 'visibility was good over route and target area, slight cloud only with a bright moon on trip – aircraft had no difficulty in identifying the target, and little or no flak was encountered'. The River Rhine, the cathedral and the bridges could easily be seen in the light of the moon and fires.

The aircraft were loaded with a mix of HE and incendiaries, with the former intended to blow the roofs off buildings so that the incendiaries could fall inside and light fires. In all, 868 aircraft (496 of which were Wellingtons) managed to attack the target successfully. Most Wellingtons attacked from between 12,000–14,000 ft. One No 9 Sqn crew reported that the 'whole town was ablaze at 0115 hrs and fires were visible 100 miles after leaving. Fires visible from the Dutch coast from 10,000 ft on return'.

Although the vast number of bombers all but overwhelmed the German defences, 29 Wellingtons failed to return from the raid. One anonymous crew was intercepted at 17,000 ft ten miles south of Eindhoven on the return leg. They described seeing 'an ME 110 carrying no lights, travelling on a reciprocal course, slightly below, to port, at a distance of approximately 200 yards. There was no searchlight or flak activity at the time and IFF had not been used. Although our aircraft took normal evasive action, altering course 30° to port and starboard alternatively, ME 110 turned and closed in to attack from the starboard quarter at same height. Our rear gunner, Sgt Dent, fired one seven-second burst at 400 yards range and enemy aircraft dived and was lost sight of temporarily.

'Five minutes later ME 110 appeared once again on the starboard quarter and attacked our aircraft, closing in from 300 yards range, firing three short bursts of both machine gun and cannon. Our rear gunner replied and claims, in which he is supported by the second pilot, to have secured "belly" hits at 80 yards range. Enemy aircraft dived from view and was not seen again. At this moment our aircraft went into an evasive dive from 17,000 ft to 12,000 ft so the enemy aircraft was not seen to crash, but it was probably damaged or destroyed.'

That night the losses included a number of OTU crews and personnel drafted in from other units to make up the numbers, including Plt Off D. M. Johnson (T2894) who had been temporarily attached to No 75 (NZ) Sqn from the Central Gunnery School at Sutton Bridge. Other aircraft were badly damaged, including Plt Off Ravenhill's X3387 from No 57 Sqn that crashed at Lakenheath on return, but the crew was safe.

After the success of the attack on Köln, the 'thousand plan' was repeated two nights later. Operation *Arabian Nights* took place on the night of 1/2 June against Essen. For this raid, the attacking force totalled 956, just short of the target figure of 1000. Most Wellington units managed to launch about 20 aircraft, and the 545 participating examples again made up more than half the force. Flt Sgt H M Goulter (Z8431) of No 12 Sqn showed remarkable skill when his port engine failed on take-off from Binbrook and he managed to crash-land his heavily-loaded bomber onto the airfield without injury to crew or setting off the 4000-lb bomb on board. Other aircraft were loaded with either one 1000- and three 500-lb HE bombs or 82 4-lb incendiaries. Four of the ten Wellingtons from No 101 Sqn were loaded with flares and the remaining six aircraft with incendiaries – the squadron was also boosted by the presence of five Wellingtons from No 23 OTU.

The bombing was more scattered this time, as the target was mostly obscured by low cloud and thick haze. The weather conditions made the searchlights ineffective, but the radar-predicted flak was as intense and accurate as ever. As Plt Off J F Summers (Z1463) of No 460 Sqn RAAF pointed out, 'operations were impeded by low cloud which increased the danger of interception by nightfighters'. His own crew witnessed 'to the north of Essen one aircraft was seen to burst into flame and go down in a slow spiral, while to the south of Essen two aircraft were seen to fall in flames'. Subsequently, as they headed for home at low level, about 20 miles north of Antwerp, the Wellington was 'held in searchlight at 500 ft. The rear gunner, Sgt T C Harris, shot down the beam of the searchlight, which was seen to waver and after a second burst was extinguished'.

Plt Off G E Murdoch (DV884) of No 75 (NZ) Sqn was chased by a Bf 109 for five minutes but managed to evade it, and Sgt Owen (DV799) of No 156 Sqn jettisoned his bombs when he was attacked by a Bf 110 near Mönchen-Gladbach. The nightfighter closed to 100 yards and fired its cannon, causing significant damage to the aircraft. Although the

WAAFs from an unidentified maintenance unit replace damaged fabric on the wing of a Wellington (*BAE Systems courtesy of Brooklands Museum*)

Wellington was able to escape by diving to 4000 ft, it was so badly shot up that the bomber crash-landed upon its return to base.

The raid on Essen was followed by a smaller follow-up attack the next night, comprising just under 200 bombers, of which half were Wellingtons. The German defences were effective and a number of Wellingtons were downed, including six crews that had operated over Essen on the previous night – Sgt Cummock (X9787) from No 57 Sqn, Plt Off T R R Wood (X3635) and Flt Sgt J L Hutchison (X3725/T) from No 115 Sqn, Sgt P D Powell (DV786) from No 156 Squadron and Sgt S Levitus (Z1249) and Plt Off J W Keene (Z1394) from No 460 Sqn RAAF.

Essen was bombed again on the nights of 5/6 and 8/9 June, and during the latter raid, luck ran out for Plt Off Murdoch and his crew, who had successfully evaded the Bf 109 a week previously. On 12 June, Wg Cdr Mellor (X3465) led a second aircraft from No 150 Sqn in daylight towards Essen. It was a very cloudy day and one aircraft dropped on the estimated time of arrival (ETA) over Essen, while the other targeted Borken.

An unfortunate incident on 18 June illustrated the many risks that RAF bomber crews faced beyond those posed by enemy action. Plt Off J G Power (W5381) of No 12 Sqn was carrying out a night flying test on his aircraft when the weather changed for the worse and the airfield was covered by low cloud. However, Power still attempted to land in these conditions, only to hit a tree and crash. He was killed and the remaining three crew were injured.

There were two nights of raids against Emden before a third 'thousand-bomber raid', Operation *Millennium II*, was launched on the night of 25/26 June. There were two possible targets depending on the weather – Duisburg and Bremen, code-named 'Salmon' and 'Cod', respectively. On the day the weather favoured Bremen, so a force of 1067 bombers, including 472 Wellingtons, was despatched to 'Cod'. This number included aircraft from OTUs, as well as Wellingtons from Coastal Command released to Bomber Command for the raid. The two units involved – Nos 304 (Polish) and 311 (Czech) Sqns – had only recently been transferred to Coastal Command. They provided 18 aircraft between them.

Despite the optimistic forecast, the weather over Bremen was cloudy. Since the target was outside the range of Gee, many aircraft were unable to find Bremen and brought their bombs back. Follow-up raids on the city were carried out on subsequent nights, and another large (325-bomber) operation followed on the night of 2/3 July. Some of the crews from No 150 Sqn, which sent 16 aircraft, stated that 'flares would have been a great help and they regretted their absence'. On the other hand, the view of the 12 No 156 Sqn crews was that the 'river and docks were clearly visible by light from gun flashes'. According to No 301 (Polish) Sqn, which sent 14 Wellingtons to Bremen on 2/3 July, 'moderate and intense heavy flak was encountered over the target. One cone and single searchlights cooperated with the flak. Moderate light flak and heavy flak was also encountered at Texel and Oldenburg with searchlight cooperation'.

For the Bomber Command Wellington squadrons, much of July was spent with mine laying sorties, although daytime cloud cover raids were also mounted. On 10 July four aircraft from No 57 Sqn headed for

Duisburg, while four from No 75 (NZ) Sqn set off for Düsseldorf. Most crews abandoned the mission because of insufficient cloud cover, but Sgt Wilmshurst (X3720) of No 75 (NZ) Sqn failed to return.

Two aircraft from No 150 Sqn, led by Wg Cdr Carter (X3465), were more successful in bombing Essen and Wesel on 16 July, and the following day the same squadron launched seven aircraft to Essen again. Four Wellingtons abandoned the mission, but two managed by 'hopping from cloud to cloud' to reach the target. The other aeroplane attacked a coastal convoy instead. A third daylight raid was mounted by No 150 Sqn on 19 July. Once again, the majority of aircraft turned back early, but one reached Essen, only for its bombs to hang up, and another Wellington failed to return.

The next day, 12 Wellingtons (six each from Nos 57 and 75 (NZ) Sqns) took off for a daylight raid on Bremen. Sgts Croston (Z1656) and Cameron (Z1653) from No 57 Sqn both bombed the target at 1620 hrs, and their squadronmate Sgt Hudson (Z1654) attacked Emden two hours later. However, all six aircraft from No 75 (NZ) Sqn abandoned the mission because of insufficient cloud. Sgt C Croall (X3452) aborted when cloud cover ran out near Emden. The crew had already fought off two fighter attacks on the outbound leg and had to run the gauntlet of two more on the return leg;

'When just north of Ameland at 1920 hrs, aircraft was flying at 4000 ft on a heading of 120 degrees. Two ME 110s were seen, one on the starboard quarter at 600 yards and one on the port bow at the same distance. Both enemy aircraft were slightly above and had apparently climbed out of cloud. One enemy aircraft turned in on the port beam. On instructions from the front gunner, Sgt W. H. Bright, captain turned to port and front gunner fired three sharp bursts at 400 yards. Enemy aircraft turned away at 300 yards without firing.

'The wireless operator, Flt Sgt J R Gratton, reported another ME 110 on starboard quarter, above at 600 yards. Rear gunner, Sgt T E Crarer, had turned turret to port to attack the first enemy aircraft and quickly fired a two-second burst. This enemy aircraft then broke away. The second enemy aircraft came in to 500 yards on starboard quarter. The rear gunner fired two three-second bursts and this enemy aircraft also turned away. During the two attacks, the captain, after turning to port, skidded away to starboard in a dive towards cloud. Both enemy aircraft had broken off attack before our aircraft reached cloud.

'Two or three minutes later, while still heading 120 degrees at 3500 ft, our aircraft came to a break in cloud and ME 110 fired at 300–400 yards from port quarter above. Rear gunner immediately replied with a four-second burst at same range. Captain dived to port and enemy aircraft was seen to break off attack as our aircraft entered cloud. During this incident our aircraft was hit by one bullet.

'A further ME 110 was encountered just northeast of Leeuwarden at 1950 hrs. Our aircraft was heading 290 degrees and at 4000 ft. The enemy aircraft was seen by the wireless operator on port quarter and above at 800 yards. As enemy aircraft approached to 400–500 yards, rear gunner fired two short bursts. Our aircraft was weaving just above the broken cloud. When rear gunner fired, enemy aircraft turned away on port side.

'When approximately 50 miles northwest of Terschelling at 2020 hrs, our aircraft was heading 290 degrees and flying at 200 ft. Wireless operator reported ME 110 at 800 yards approaching from port quarter at sea level. Enemy aircraft flew parallel course on port side and our aircraft went down to sea level. Rear gunner fired three short bursts at 300 yards which forced enemy aircraft up. As enemy aircraft climbed, wireless operator opened fire with beam gun, but owing to a stoppage only got in a very short burst. Enemy aircraft did a climbing turn and came in from port bow at 400 yards. As enemy aircraft came in, captain turned to port. Front gunner fired continuously from 300 yards to point blank as enemy aircraft passed over our aircraft at 50 ft above from port bow to astern. Rear gunner fired a final burst of four seconds at close range. As enemy aircraft was lost astern, smoke was seen coming from the port engine. This enemy aircraft appeared to be a nightfighter as it was painted black.'

Sgt Croall and his crew were shot down and captured eight days later on a raid on Hamburg.

Duisburg had been attacked for three consecutive nights before Hamburg was bombed on 26/27 and again on 28/29 July. The frontline squadrons were augmented by OTU crews for the second raid, and also for the raid on the following night by 630 aircraft (including 308 Wellingtons) against Düsseldorf. On this mission OC No 101 Sqn, Wg Cdr A C Vautour (BJ841), was shot down. Mine laying sorties and raids against Osnabrück, Mainz and Düsseldorf were carried out in the first fortnight of August.

The night of 18/19 August saw the first operation by the new Pathfinder Force (PFF), which included No 156 Sqn Wellingtons that had moved to a new base at Warboys. Only two of the eight PFF Wellingtons were loaded with flares, and Flt Sgt T E Case (BJ600), in the second flare aircraft, discovered that a flare had ignited in the bomb-bay just after take-off. The rest of the flares were hastily jettisoned, but they still caught alight, falling near a farm five miles from the airfield without causing any damage. Despite the efforts of the PFF, a thick haze in the target area meant this mission enjoyed only limited success.

As the German defences continued to improve, so the casualty rate amongst the Wellington force increased. During the operation against Kassel on 27/28 August 21 Wellingtons were lost, five of them from No 142 Sqn, which had launched 15 aircraft that night. The PFF Wellingtons of No 156 Sqn comprised two flare aircraft, five marker bombers loaded with incendiaries only and nine more aircraft loaded with HE bombs. There was a thick ground haze, and No 150 Sqn noted that there were 'conflicting reports on the efficiency of the PFF'. Surviving crews from No 142 Sqn reported that the flares had been dropped as much as 20 miles west of the target, and that haze prevented them from pinpointing most of the fires on arrival in the target area. There were also heavy losses amongst the Wellington crews who attacked Nürnburg on 28/29 August, including Flt Lt W Gilmour (X3728) from No 156 Sqn PFF on his 47th operational mission.

During the month of August No 460 Sqn RAAF re-equipped with the Halifax, but No 425 Sqn RCAF was formed at Dishforth and another Article XV unit, No 420 Sqn RCAF, started its conversion from the

Hampden to the Wellington. In September, both Nos 9 and 57 Sqns would re-equip with the Lancaster.

Late 1942 also saw the introduction of the Vickers Type 448 Wellington X into frontline service. It was similar in configuration to the Wellington III, but powered by two 1675-hp Bristol Hercules VI or XVI engines. Taking advantage of newly-developed light aluminium alloys instead of steel, the structure was strengthened to allow a maximum take-off weight of 36,500 lbs. Between them, the factories at Blackpool and Chester built 3803 Wellington Xs, making it the most numerous version of the Wellington. Carrying a full bomb load of 4500 lbs, it had a range of 1325 miles flying at 255 mph at 15,000 ft. The Wellington X was used in Bomber Command for both operations and training, and it also served in large numbers in both the Middle East and the Far East.

There were three raids during September that used the Operation *Grand National* augmentation of the frontline squadrons by OTU crews. On the night of 10/11 September, the main force of 478 bombers that attacked Düsseldorf included a substantial number of Wellington OTU crews. However, losses were high – No 16 OTU lost five of 13 Wellingtons despatched. The OTUs also took part in main force operations over Bremen on 13/14 September and Essen on 16/17 September.

The mine laying campaign continued throughout the autumn months, and the experiences of No 420 Sqn RCAF on the night of 26/27 November are perhaps typical. The weather was poor and only two of six aircraft were successful in finding their 'garden', code-named 'Jellyfish', on the approaches to Saint-Nazaire. Flt Lt L S Anderson (BK235) reported that 'we flew in and out of 8/10ths cloud over England. The trip out in the Channel was below 10/10ths cloud and we were unable to see. I flew on for another hour, and due to the lack of Gee fixes I assumed that we would be unable to pinpoint the islands in such conditions. Thus, knowing that we couldn't drop our mines on Dead Reckoning I turned and set course for Predannack'. On the other hand, Sqn Ldr D S Jacobs (BK295) found that 'weather on the trip was exceedingly poor until Belle Isle was reached. Over garden, bright moonlight and no cloud made pinpointing fairly easy. Vegetables definitely in correct position'.

The Wellington X prototype X3595 was photographed at Brooklands in May 1942 while still sporting the markings of No 75 (NZ) Sqn, with whom it had briefly served in March 1942 (*BAE Systems courtesy of Brooklands Museum*)

The daylight cloud cover raids continued, too, and on 22 October 22 Wellingtons were sent against Essen, with varying success – two aircraft from No 75 (NZ) Sqn bombed under a 700-ft cloud base. Sometimes there was too much cloud, and aircraft dropped their ordnance in the midst of it on the ETA over the target, which was unlikely to result in accurate bombing. This technique was used by Flt Sgt C P Lundeen (BJ717) of No 420 Sqn against Krefeld on 23 October and three aircraft from No 419 Sqn against Emden 24 hours later. Meanwhile, the

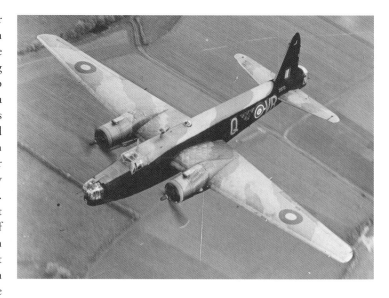

Wellington Mk III Z1572 was damaged on the night of 14/15 April 1942 while serving with No 75 (NZ) Sqn. After repairs, it was issued to No 419 Sqn RCAF, whose markings it is seen in here. The squadron re-equipped with the Halifax II in October 1942 (*Philip Jarrett*)

targets attacked during night operations included Osnabrück, Kiel and Köln, as well as Genoa on 23/24 October. The latter force included 18 Wellingtons, eight from No 75 (NZ) Sqn and ten from No 115 Sqn. These aircraft had to descend below a 3000–4000 ft cloud base to drop their bombs. The following night Milan was targeted, and three Wellingtons from No 75 (NZ) Sqn and one from No 115 Sqn failed to return.

The last quarter of 1942 marked a shift away from the Wellington being the pre-eminent aircraft type operated by Bomber Command. The operation against Stuttgart on the night of 22/23 November was remarkable in being the first raid by Bomber Command in which Wellingtons did not make up the majority of the attacking force. Although Wellington squadrons continued to represent a substantial proportion of the frontline strength of Bomber Command, a steady stream of units converted from the Wellington onto four-engined 'heavies', while others deployed to the Middle East theatre.

In October No 101 Sqn converted to the Lancaster, as did No 12 Sqn in November. That same month No 75 (NZ) Sqn re-equipped with the Stirling and No 419 Sqn RCAF with the Halifax. On 9 December, 13 Wellingtons each from Nos 142 and 150 Sqns flew to Portreath and thence out to the Middle East. However, the rear echelons of both units were amalgamated to form No 166 Sqn in January 1943. In the same timescale, more new squadrons were also formed with the Wellington, although the type was seen as an interim aeroplane until sufficient four-engined bombers became available. No 199 Sqn formed at Ingham and No 196 Sqn at Leconfield in November and December, respectively.

Perhaps more importantly, a significant number of Article XV units were formed, including No 466 Sqn RAAF at Driffield in October and, over the next three months, no less than six RCAF squadrons. The expansion of the RCAF bomber force coincided with the formation of a separate group, No 6 (RCAF) Group, to command these units. By the beginning of January 1943, the Air Order of Battle of Wellington squadrons in Bomber Command was as follows;

The crew of Wellington IV Z1407 of No 300 (Polish) Sqn pose for the camera alongside their badly damaged bomber upon returning from a mission to Bremen in September 1942. They are, from left to right, Flt Sgt Tomiec, Plt Off Z Brzezinski, Flg Off Machej, WO K Muszynski and Flt Lt Bilinski (*Wellington Aviation*)

No 1 Group

Kirmington	No 166 Sqn (AS)
Ingham	No 199 Sqn (EX)
Helmswell	No 300 (Polish) Sqn (BH)
	No 301 (Polish) Sqn (GR)
	No 305 (Polish) Sqn (SM)

No 3 Group

East Wretham	No 115 Sqn (KO)
Warboys	No 156 Sqn (GT)

No 4 Group

Leconfield	No 196 Sqn (ZO)
East Moor	No 429 Sqn RCAF (AL)
Burn	No 431 Sqn RCAF (SE)
Driffield	No 466 Sqn RAAF (HD)

No 6 (RCAF) Group

Middleton St George	No 420 Sqn RCAF (PT)
Topcliffe	No 424 Sqn RCAF (QB)
Dishforth	No 425 Sqn RCAF (KW)
	No 426 Sqn RCAF (OW)
Croft	No 427 Sqn RCAF (ZL)
Dalton	No 428 Sqn RCAF (NA)

As well as its primary bomber role, the inherent flexibility of the Wellington design made it an ideal platform for other 'special duties'. Much of the development work for the Gee navigation system in 1942 had been carried out by high-altitude Wellington Vs and VIs of No 109 Sqn, although these were replaced by Mosquitoes for operational sorties over Germany. Furthermore, when No 161 Sqn formed at Newmarket in 1942 for work with the Special Operations Executive, it included a Wellington that was used for radio interception work. Similarly, No 192 Sqn, which formed at Gransden Lodge in January 1943 by the amalgamation of Nos 1473 and 1474 Wireless Investigation Flights, was equipped with Wellingtons.

During January 1943, Wellingtons were excluded from main force bomber operations over Germany and used instead mostly for mine laying. However, the attack on the U-Boat base at Lorient on the night 14/15 January included 33 Wellingtons. Nine aircraft from No 156 Sqn, led by Sqn Ldr S G Hookway (BK508), marked the target with flares and incendiaries on the last Wellington mission mounted by the squadron before it converted to Lancasters. This was also the first bombing mission by No 6 (RCAF) Group, and it included the first loss of a group aircraft when Plt Off G Milne (BK165) of No 426 Sqn RCAF failed to return. Lorient was also bombed on 26/27 and 29/30 January.

A daylight raid was also mounted against Oldenburg by three Wellingtons from No 420 Sqn on 30 January in one of the last cloud cover raids by the type. Two aircraft turned back and Flt Lt R H Lowe (X1680) failed to return, having sent out a distress call that the aircraft had ditched. Night attacks on the U-Boat pens at Lorient continued through February, including the first operation by No 196 Sqn when Wg Cdr R H Waterhouse (HK168) led nine Wellingtons on 4/5 February. Other raids against Lorient were mounted on 7/8, 13/14 and 16/17 February.

The Wellington squadrons returned to Germany in March, participating in raids on Hamburg and Essen early in the month. Four Wellingtons from No 115 Sqn took part in the raid on Essen on 12/13 March and Sgt L Fallon (BJ756) failed to return. This was the final Wellington operation undertaken by No 115 Sqn, the last of the original units equipped with the aircraft since 1939 – it received Lancasters in April. More squadron re-equipment followed over the next few months. No 301 (Polish) Sqn disbanded in April, but in May No 432 Sqn RCAF formed at Skipton-on-Swale and Nos 420, 424, 425 Sqns RCAF all deployed to the Middle East. Two other Canadian Wellington units, Nos 427 and 428 Sqns RCAF, re-equipped with the Halifax in May and June.

During the first half of 1943, the Wellingtons of No 6 (RCAF) Group were heavily involved in operations over Germany, including raids on Kiel on 4/5 April, Frankfurt on 10/11 April and Dortmund on 4/5 May and 23/24 May. During the latter raid, Flt Lt C H Hall (HE198) of No 431 Sqn RCAF was caught in searchlights and the aircraft damaged by flak. After an unsuccessful dive in an attempt to break away from the searchlights, the pilot called over the intercom, 'I think we ought to bail out' and then promptly did so(!), as did the rear gunner, Sgt C A McD Warne. However, the rest of the crew remained on board and the bomb aimer, Sgt S N Sloan, took control of the aircraft. Despite the forward hatch and the rear turret door being open, which caused a strong draught to blow through the fuselage, Sloan, navigator Sgt G C W Parslow and wireless operator Flg Off J B G Bailey managed to recover the aircraft to a safe landing at Cranwell. Sloan was awarded the Conspicuous Gallantry Medal for his courage.

The aircrew of No 196 Sqn photographed in front of a Wellington X at Leconfield in early 1943. The unit had formed the previous November and converted to Stirling IIIs at Witchford in July 1943 (*RAF Museum*)

In the first half of 1943, the number of Wellington squadrons in Bomber Command diminished significantly, and by 30 June the Air Order of Battle comprised the following units;

No 1 Group

Kirmington	No 166 Sqn (AS)
Hemswell	No 300 (Polish) Sqn (BH)
	No 305 (Polish) Sqn (SM)
Lakenheath	No 199 Sqn (EX)

No 4 Group

Leconfield	No 196 Sqn (ZO)
	No 466 Sqn RAAF (HD)

Immaculate-looking Presentation Wellington III BK398 *GOLD COAST* of No 424 Sqn RCAF basks in the sunshine at Topcliffe in late 1942. The aircraft was later transferred to No 26 OTU after the squadron received Wellington Xs from February 1943 (*Philip Jarrett*)

No 6 (RCAF) Group

Linton-on-Ouse	No 426 Sqn RCAF (OW)
East Moor	No 429 Sqn RCAF (AL)
Burn	No 431 Sqn RCAF (SE)
Skipton-on-Swale	No 432 Sqn RCAF (QO)

Over the next few months, most of these units also gave up their Wellingtons for more modern types. July saw No 426 Sqn RCAF convert to the Lancaster and both Nos 196 and 199 Sqns switch to the Stirling. The following month No 429 Sqn RCAF converted to the Halifax, and in September No 166 Sqn re-equipped with the Lancaster, No 305 (Polish) Sqn with the Mitchell II and No 466 Sqn RAAF with the Halifax.

For much of the summer the Wellington units had concentrated on mine laying, although a steadily decreasing number of aircraft had also been participating in main bomber force raids over Germany. While other units were re-equipped, No 300 (Polish) Sqn soldiered on with its Wellingtons. The last main force bomber operation by Wellingtons was the raid on Hanover on 8/9 October, with 26 aircraft from No 300 (Polish) Sqn and No 432 Sqn RCAF taking part. Amongst the former were 12 Wellington Xs, although two returned early, one because of fighter attack and the other due to overheating engines. The remainder bombed red and green Target Indicator markers from 18,000 ft.

After this operation, No 432 Sqn RCAF converted to Lancasters, but No 300 (Polish) Sqn continued to fly the Wellington on mine laying sorties for the next five months. The squadron sowed its 2000th mine on 30 November 1943, and it carried on in this role into 1944. The last operational sortie by a frontline Bomber Command Wellington squadron was a mine laying sortie off Lorient by No 300 (Polish) Sqn on the night of 3/4 March 1944. Later that month the unit converted to the Lancaster.

Groundcrew work on No 300 (Polish) Sqn's Wellington Xs at Hemswell while another aircraft from the unit performs a low-level pass over the flightline in June 1943. The aircraft closest to the camera has been adorned with a dwarf motif, which is pointing to the Polish air force chequerboard marking below the cockpit. This unit would fly four marks of Wellington bomber until finally converting the Lancaster I in March 1944 (*Wojtek Matusiak*)

CHAPTER FIVE

TRAINING

A Wellington I of No 11 OTU performs an impressive beat-up of Bassingbourn in July 1940 (*Wellington Aviation*)

U ntil early 1940, the conversion of aircrew posted from flying training schools was carried out by reserve squadrons in each group. Within No 3 Group, operational training was delivered by Nos 75 and 148 Sqns at Harwell and No 215 Sqn at Bassingbourn. At Harwell, No 148 Sqn was responsible for conversions to type and navigation training, while No 75 Sqn carried out armament and operational training.

However, it was clear to AOC-in-C Bomber Command, Air Chief Marshal Sir E R Ludlow-Hewitt, that a more robust system was needed, especially if Bomber Command was to be expanded. Under his direction, a formal system of OTUs was introduced to bridge the gap between flying training schools and operational squadrons. In April 1940 No 6 Group was established, with responsibility for operational training within Bomber Command, and the first OTUs were formed under its auspices. These included two Wellington conversion units, Nos 11 and 15 OTUs, which were formed from the original No 3 Group Reserve squadrons at Bassingbourn and Harwell, respectively.

Each OTU was a large unit, as evidenced by the fact that No 15 OTU was formed on 8 April by amalgamating the two squadrons at Harwell. Whereas an operational squadron had an establishment of 16 Wellingtons, plus two more In-Use Reserves (IURs), the establishment of an OTU was 40 Wellingtons and 14 IURs, as well as 14 Ansons and four Anson IURs. So, in terms of aircraft numbers alone, each OTU was the equivalent strength of four operational squadrons. The corollary of this was that staffing and, to a certain extent, equipping the OTUs represented a huge drain of frontline resources. Both the sheer number of aeroplanes and the nature of the training task also meant that a single airfield was inadequate for a whole OTU. Therefore, each OTU was split into two flights over a main base and a satellite airfield. As the war progressed and the training load increased, additional OTUs were formed and more airfields needed to be constructed. The OTU system, therefore, represented a massive commitment in personnel, logistics and equipment.

In June 1940, the Air Order of Battle of Wellington OTUs was;

No 6 Group

Bassingbourn/Steeple Morden	No 11 OTU (KH, KJ, LG, OP, TX)
Harwell/Hampstead Norris	No 15 OTU (EO, FH, KK)

Initially, the OTU course lasted a nominal eight weeks, consisting of a one-week ground school followed by a 55-hour flying syllabus. In fact, the eight-week timescale only worked in the summer, and more realistic times were ten weeks in the spring and autumn and as long as 12 weeks in the winter. Furthermore, since not all of the sorties were flown as a constituted crew, it took about 90 flying hours to train a complete crew.

The ground school phase of the course made use of synthetic training, with pilots flying about eight hours in Link Trainer flight simulators and wireless operators spending time in the Harwell Box – a representation of the wireless compartment, complete with engine noise – practising sending and receiving messages. For bomb aimers, the Air Ministry Laboratories trainer involved a bombsight mounted on a platform, with film of the ground being projected onto the floor below to simulate flight over a target. The Turret Gun Sighting Trainer for gunners also made use of projected film of attacking fighters.

For pilots, the Wellington represented a huge step up from the Oxford or Anson trainers that they had become accustomed to at flying training school. Each pilot received a 12–16-hour conversion to type, followed by 29–33 hours of operational training. For navigators/observers and air gunners, the allocation was 58–66 hours of flying, but in the case of wireless operator/air gunners (WOpAGs), the 66 flying hours were split evenly between working the radio set and the gun turret. With courses starting every two weeks in the summer, the pupil population of a typical OTU was around 104 pilots, 104 WOpAGs, 52 navigators and 52 air gunners.

Pilot, navigator and air gunner pupils arrived at the OTU from their specialist training courses having had little or no contact with other crew specialisations. One of the first tasks was to transform a large number of individuals into a small number of constituted crews, and OTUs took slightly different approaches to this task. However, they all essentially entailed the pupils sorting themselves into crews within the first week, rather than applying any scientific method of matching skills and personalities. The resulting crew constitutions worked well for most aircrew, but proved disastrous for others.

Instructors were drawn from 'screened' crews – those who had successfully completed a 30-mission tour of operations and had earned a rest tour. With a limited supply of screened crews and a rising demand for instructors, the quality of instruction at the OTUs was variable. So, too, was the quality of aircraft, for frontline squadrons had first call on new airframes and the OTUs often had to make do with tired bombers that had been flown hard on operational sorties. Engines, in particular, tended to have become de-rated over time and were not able to reliably produce full power. At the end of 1941 there were still 50 original Wellington Is still in service with OTUs, which at the time were deemed by the AOC No 6 Group, Air Commodore W F MacNeece Foster, to be 'very old and difficult to keep serviceable'.

As at Harwell in the days of Nos 75 and 148 Sqns, the OTU syllabus was split between the two flights, with one concentrating on conversion to type and basic navigation practice and the other on operational profiles, including bombing and gunnery. In the Basic Flight, conversion flying started with circuit and instrument flying for the pilots, with both the first and second pilot taking their turn. Once pilots were cleared to fly the Wellington without supervision from an instructor, the crew practised working together as a team during navigation sorties. Basic navigation training included daylight cross-country flights of increasing length and complexity and an introduction to night work.

In the Advanced Flight crews practised bombing techniques using 10-lb smoke bombs by day and 11.5-lb flash bombs at night. The range at Radway, in Warwickshire, was typical of the facilities used by the OTUs. The aiming point was a triangle within a 50-ft circle, which was illuminated at night by electric lights. In two quadrant towers, airmen would plot the relative bearing of each bomb strike, with their readings telephoned through to the OTU staff to assess the accuracy of the bombing.

Another method to measure bombing accuracy at certain ranges was by means of an infrared searchlight, which was aligned along the line of the bombing run and aimed upwards towards the correct release point. When using this system, no practice weapons were dropped, but the camera on board the aircraft photographed the instant that the bomb aimer pressed the release button. If the run was accurate, there would be a trace from the infrared light on the photograph. This system was used during 'Bullseye' sorties in the latter part of the course. A Bullseye exercise was a simulated bombing mission during which the crew had to find their way at night to the target (an infrared range near Conwy, in North Wales, for example) and return to base. After completion of the requisite number of Bullseye sorties, the crew could expect to be tasked with a live 'nickelling' sortie over France as their final trip of the OTU course.

By the end of 1940, there were three more Wellington OTUs. No 12 OTU had been formed to teach Battle crews at Benson and Mount Farm in April by the amalgamation of Nos 52 and 63 Sqns and 'C' Flight of No 12 Sqn, but with the demise of the aircraft in No 1 Group, the unit had converted to the Wellington in December 1940. Another Battle OTU that re-equipped with the Wellington was No 18 (Polish) OTU – a half-strength unit formed at Hucknell in May 1940 in order to train émigré Polish aircrew. With the fall of France, there was a steady flow of Poles wanting to join the RAF. In September 1940 the first No 18 OTU

Wellington IA N2892 of No 11 OTU had survived the ill-fated Wilhelmshaven raid of 18 December 1939 while serving with No 149 Sqn (*Graham Pitchfork*)

course commenced with ten pilots, 13 observers and 19 air gunners. The unit moved to Bramcote in January 1941, where it also used Bitteswell as a satellite airfield, and where it was to expand to full strength. The third unit was No 20 OTU, formed on 27 May at Lossiemouth, with a satellite at Elgin.

In parallel with the Bomber Command OTUs, Coastal Command formed its own OTUs to train Wellington crews for the maritime patrol and anti-submarine warfare roles.

By January 1941 the Air Order of Battle of Wellington OTUs in Bomber Command was;

No 6 Group

Bassingbourn/Steeple Morden	No 11 OTU (KH, KJ, LG, OP, TX)
Benson/Mount Farm	No 12 OTU (FQ, JP, ML)
Harwell/Hampstead Norris	No 15 OTU (EO, FH, KK)
Bramcote/Bitteswell	No 18 (Polish) OTU (EN, VQ, XW)
Lossiemouth/Elgin	No 20 OTU (AI, HJ, JM, MK, XL, YR, ZT)

The expansion of Bomber Command in 1941–42 was reflected in a commensurate expansion in the OTUs. Indeed, any increase in the number of operational squadrons had to be preceded by enlarging the training system in order to provide the requisite new crews. As ever, the drain on the resources of the frontline to provide instructors was a limiting factor. Writing in January 1941, Air Marshal Sir R E C Peirse, AOC-in-C Bomber Command, wrote 'the suggestion to form ten new Heavy OTUs between March and June would necessitate the withdrawal of 600 pilots from operational squadrons to form the screened staff. This 600 would be taken from an establishment of 1120 British pilots, and would therefore be reducing our operational squadrons by more than 50 per cent'.

Furthermore, since No 1 Group squadrons were at half strength and were still in the process of conversion and training, no pilots could be spared from them. No 3 Group squadrons were also short of 68 pilots and had a commitment to provide 42 Wellington pilots to the Middle East by the end of January 1941, followed by 18 pilots per month thereafter. Peirse proposed, therefore, a more modest expansion of the OTUs. He suggested that reducing the manpower in No 3 Group's squadrons to 15 crews each would generate a surplus of 100 pilots, and that a further 50 could be sourced from across Nos 4 and 5 Groups. In this way, 150 pilots could be found, or enough for three new Wellington OTUs. It was anticipated that as they came on line, each OTU would produce 24 crews per month.

The new Wellington OTUs were to be formed at newly-built airfields at Moreton-in-Marsh, Pershore and Lichfield. In addition, another Whitley OTU was to be formed at Wellesbourne Mountford and a Hampden OTU at Chipping Warden. Most of these airfields were still under construction, so the expansion of the OTUs was a huge undertaking. In the meantime, in view of the fact that a Hampden OTU was to be set up in Canada and no more Whitley squadrons were to be formed, the decision was taken that the OTUs based at Wellesbourne Mountford and Chipping Warden would also be equipped with Wellingtons. The first airfield to be available for use was Moreton-in-Marsh, and No 21 OTU started training there on 15 March. This was followed by No 23 OTU at Pershore on 1 April.

Unfortunately, it took slightly longer than anticipated for the new airfields to be fully completed, and on 5 April it was announced that 'because of the backward state of aerodromes, dispersal points etc., which makes it impossible to operate full numbers of aircraft', the establishment of the new OTUs would be filled to only 75 per cent. Thus, the four OTUs would, in effect, produce the output of three. On 1 May, No 22 OTU started training at Wellesbourne Mountford, and No 27 OTU followed suit at Lichfield three weeks later.

Flying training in wartime was not without risk, and there were six fatal accidents involving OTU Wellingtons in April 1941 alone. Most occurred in the dark, and some simply reflected the risks associated with inexperience and flying at night. Plt Off H H Boler (L4302) of No 11 OTU and Plt Off R J Hawkes (L4297) of No 18 OTU both crashed while practising night circuits on 18 and 29 April, respectively. However, other accidents were the direct result of wartime conditions. On 24 April Sgt P N Nicholls (N2912) of No 11 OTU was downed by a Do 17 night intruder while on night circuit training at Bassingbourn. The aircraft crashed onto the airfield and hit the Wellington of Sgt F N Alstrom (R1404), which was parked on a dispersal pan. Although Nicholls survived the ordeal, all other crewmen were killed. On 30 April Plt Off K G Evans (T2905) of No 11 OTU became lost on a night cross-country exercise and flew into barrage balloon cables over Bristol, causing the aircraft to crash with the deaths of the entire crew.

The OTU syllabus was constantly under review, not least because of the growing demands of the frontline

A No 21 OTU Wellington makes an approach at Moreton-in-Marsh over the wreckage of Mk IA N2845, which had crashed on the airfield boundary in September 1941 (*Wellington Aviation*)

bomber force. At a conference of his OTU commanders in April 1941, the AOC No 6 Group described that there was an 'urgent necessity for increasing the flow of our pilots. At the same time, it is essential not to increase the number of OTUs, since the present number entails a very heavy strain on our expansion programme for operational squadrons on the frontline'. The solution to this quandary was that while 'previously the length of time spent at the controls by pilots under training had been 55 hours, now it is proposed to reduce this period to a minimum of 30 hours'.

Pilots graduated from the OTU course as qualified aircraft captains, but when they arrived at their operational Wellington squadron they became second pilots to an operationally experienced captain. The revised syllabus involved an 18-hour conversion phase for pilots, followed by 12 hours of operational training. This almost exactly reversed the balance of flying on the original course, but it reflected the need for second pilots to be fully confident in the handling of the aircraft, since they would get less flying practice as second pilots. Additionally, they would effectively have an apprenticeship in operational flying while on live missions.

Course reports from No 15 OTU at Harwell during 1941 give a good flavour of the courses. In describing No 38 Course, which started on 1 June and graduated on 14 July, the chief instructor wrote 'the general flying standard of the pilots was average, but three captains were above average. Ten crews successfully completed a Nickel mission. Two 250-lb bombs were carried on these operations, but the majority of crews were unable to locate an enemy aerodrome to strafe and the bombs were brought back. The remaining two crews, owing to bad weather conditions, were unable to carry out a Nickel operation. In lieu of this they completed a seven-hour cross-country flight to NW Scotland. This cross-country was successfully completed in adverse weather conditions, the crews obtaining valuable experience in bad weather flying'.

Two months later, No 41 Course graduated, and the report described it as 'being characterized by the great keenness of all the crews and the extreme mediocrity of its pilots. These pilots were all very keen and conscientious and anxious to get on with the job. They were fine types, and no hours of work seemed too long for them. Their main concern was to get their training done as quickly as possible, and they cooperated extremely well with the staff. Had their flying capabilities been up to their other standard this would have been an exceptional course. Owing to the wear and tear on our aircraft in an attempt to get them up to standard, our serviceability fell off to such an extent that the training of crews 1 to 6 did not proceed with the desired smoothness, as the brunt of the unserviceability fell upon them'.

As well as Poles, a number of Czechoslovakian nationals continued to enlist in the RAF. Initially, they received training within No 311 (Czech) Sqn, but in December 1941 No 1429 Czech Operational Training Flight was created, flying Wellingtons. The flight was initially based at East Wretham and later at North Luffenham.

By the end of December 1941, the 21 frontline Wellington squadrons within Bomber Command were being supported by nine OTUs;

No 6 Group

Bassingbourn/Steeple Morden	No 11 OTU (KH, KJ, LG, OP, TX)
Chipping Warden/Gaydon	No 12 OTU (FQ, JP, ML)
Harwell/Mount Farm	No 15 OTU (EO, FH, KK)
Bramcote/Bitteswell	No 18 (Polish) OTU (EN, VQ, XW)
Lossiemouth/Elgin	No 20 OTU (AI, HJ, JM, MK, XL, YR, ZT)
Moreton-in-Marsh/Edgehill	No 21 OTU (ED, SJ, UH)
Wellesbourne Mountford/Stratford	No 22 OTU (DD, LT, OX, XN)
Pershore/Defford	No 23 OTU (BY, FZ, WE)
Lichfield/Tattenhall	No 27 OTU (BB, UJ, YC, YL)

The pressure to provide increasing numbers of qualified Wellington crews to fill empty spaces in the expanding frontline continued through the winter of 1941. There was pressure from the other direction, too, as the flying training schools were producing pilots more quickly than they could be assimilated into the OTU system. By January 1942 there were 78 surplus pilots awaiting an OTU course. In the same month, Air Commodore MacNeece Foster wrote that 'the opinion has recently been expressed that OTUs will produce crews punctually to a given timetable if pressure is brought to bear on them. The Inspector General quoted in a recent report that this had proved to be the case at Harwell. This is in fact possible up to a point, and this method was resorted to at No 21 OTU Moreton last month.

'Success has, however, only been achieved by keeping these OTUs fully up to strength in both aircraft and screened personnel. This has been done at the expense of other OTUs. Forcing the pace in this manner has had a marked effect on casualties at both these stations, the increase in the crash rate at Moreton rising from ten accidents in October and November to a total of 12 for the month of December alone.'

At that time there was also growing demand for Wellington crews in the Middle East theatre, and the two OTUs mentioned by MacNeece Foster, Nos 15 and 21 OTUs, began to train crews exclusively for overseas deployment.

Wellington IC DV511 of No 23 OTU making an approach at dusk (*Philip Jarrett*)

Some of the pressure was taken off the OTUs when the decision was taken in March 1942 that heavy bombers should have only one pilot, since most frontline aircraft had only one set of flying controls. At once the new policy relieved the training load at the OTUs and released more screened pilots for instructional duties.

During the first half of 1942 four more Wellington OTUs were formed – No 26 OTU at Wing, No 28 OTU at Wymeswold, No 29 OTU at North Luffenham and No 30 OTU at Hixon. Additionally, No 16 OTU at Upper Heyford converted from the Hampden to the Wellington in April. In view of the growing administrative task in running the OTUs, No 6 Group was disbanded in May 1942 and its responsibilities were divided between two new training groups, Nos 91 and 92 Groups. With half of the total Wellington strength of Bomber Command allocated to training duties, the aircraft of these two groups were needed for operations in order to provide the critical number of 1000 aircraft for Operation *Millennium* at the end of May 1942.

Just over 1000 bombers attacked Köln on the night of 30/31 May 1942, of which 228 were Wellingtons from OTUs. From Chipping Warden, No 12 OTU despatched 22 aircraft, and another 30 were sent from No 15 OTU (of which 20 were from Harwell and ten from Hampstead Norris). In addition to its Hampdens, No 16 OTU launched 14 Wellingtons from Upper Heyford. Sixteen Wellingtons were sent from No 18 OTU at Bramcote, No 21 OTU despatched 22 aircraft (11 each came from Moreton-in-Marsh and Edgehill) and No 22 OTU provided 25 (14 of them from Wellesbourne Mountford and 11 from Stratford). Additionally, ten Wellingtons from No 21 OTU were detached to operate with No 150 Sqn from Snaith and another ten Wellingtons from No 22 OTU were detached to operate from Elsham Wolds. Nineteen Wellingtons came from No 23 OTU at Pershore, which also detached 15 of its aircraft to operate from Stradishall, Oakington and Bourn. Twenty Wellingtons were provided by No 26 OTU at Wing and 21 from No 27 OTU at Lichfield. The operational training units also included No 1429 Czech Operational Training Flight, which provided six Wellingtons for the raid.

Inevitably some aircraft were lost on these missions, including one from No 1429 Flight, four from No 22 OTU and three from No 26 OTU. At Snaith, the No 150 Sqn Operations Record Book recorded that 'all [21 OTU] crews unanimous in their reports concerning the success of the raid. Individual results were hard to observe owing to the smoke from the numerous fires but all crews are confident that they located their target. Without doubt tonight's effort may be regarded as an outstanding success'.

OTUs were in action again for the second *Millennium* raid to Essen, and most were able to repeat the commitment of 30 May. For example, No 22 OTU despatched 12 Wellingtons from Wellesbourne Mountford, 13 from Stratford (all of which were crewed by pupils) and nine from Elsham Wolds. Losses were relatively light, but included Flt Sgt F B Albright (W5618) of No 21 OTU. OTU crews were also used on the third 'thousand-bomber raid' against Bremen on 25/26 June.

At the end of June 1942, the Air Order of Battle of the Wellington within Bomber Command OTUs comprised 14 training units;

Wellington IC DV839 of No 21 OTU looking sorry for itself. As part of Operation *Grand National*, this aircraft augmented the Bomber Command Main Force when it targeted Düsseldorf on the night of 31 July/1 August 1942. Its crew reported being engaged by one or two Ju 88s at 0145 hrs and gunners claimed one nightfighter destroyed five miles east of Dordrecht, in western Holland. DV839 was subsequently repaired and issued to No 14 OTU at Market Harborough, with whom it was written off in a fatal crash on the night of 24 October 1943 during a cross-country training exercise. The aircraft hit the ground near Wittering airfield, killing three of the five crew (*Wellington Aviation*)

No 91 Group

Bassingbourn/Steeple Morden	No 11 OTU (KH, KJ, LG, OP, TX)
Chipping Warden/Gaydon	No 12 OTU (FQ, JP, ML)
Harwell/Grove	No 15 OTU (EO, FH, KK)
Bramcote/Bitteswell	No 18 (Polish) OTU (EN, VQ, XW)
Lossiemouth/Elgin	No 20 OTU (AI, HJ, JM, MK, XL, YR, ZT)
Moreton-in-Marsh/Edgehill	No 21 OTU (ED, SJ, UH)
Wellesbourne Mountford/Stratford	No 22 OTU (DD, LT, OX, XN)
Pershore/Defford	No 23 OTU (BY, FZ, WE)
Lichfield/Tattenhall	No 27 OTU (BB, UJ, YC, YL)

No 92 Group

Upper Heyford/Barford St John	No 16 OTU (GA, JS, XG)
Wing/Oakley	No 26 OTU (EU, PB, WG)
Wymeswold/Castle Donington	No 28 OTU (LB, QN, WY)
North Luffenham/Woolfox Lodge	No 29 OTU (TF)
Hixon/Seighford	No 30 OTU (BT, KD, TN)

Under Operation *Grand National*, the OTUs were used to augment the Bomber Command Main Force on a number of occasions during the second half of 1942. Targets included Hamburg on the night of 28/29 July, Düsseldorf on the night of 31 July/1 August and again on 10/11 September. Eighteen crews (13 from Stratford and five from Gaydon) were provided by No 22 OTU for the raid on 10/11 September, and two student crews, captained by Sgts J D Williams (R1616) and D L Pablo (X9932) failed to return from the mission. Two more raids were carried out that month, against Bremen on 13/14 September and Essen three nights later.

With the formation of No 93 Group in January 1943, there were three groups to command and administer the growing number of Wellington OTUs. In August 1942, No 14 OTU at Cottesmore had converted from the Hampden to the Wellington, No 17 OTU at Silverstone was due to convert from the Blenheim in April 1943 and No 82 OTU to form at Ossington in June. This made a total of 17 Wellington OTUs within Bomber Command.

Meanwhile, the training task continued unabated, but as ever, the dangers of war were never far away. On the night of 26/27 January 1943 instructor pilot Flg Off F H Mitchell (X9667) with No 21 OTU took off with a crew of seven for a Bullseye sortie that involved routing outwards over the North Sea to a point 50 miles off Clacton before returning home. The Wellington must have strayed from its route, because it was downed by a nightfighter over the Dutch coast. Six crew were killed and air gunner Flt Sgt J N Morgan taken prisoner. He later reported that 'Flg Off Frank Mitchell, our Captain and pilot, remained at the controls, giving myself and others the opportunity of abandoning the aircraft in the nick of time. The suddenness of the attack that ended our ill-fated flight was such that I am unable to give much detail of our last moments together'.

Weather also continued to be a hazard to inexperienced crews. On 29/30 January three Wellingtons from OTUs were lost in three fatal accidents in the Peak District on the same night. Flg Off A W Lane (R1011) and Sgt G A Reynolds (R1538) were amongst seven aircraft from No 28 OTU at Wymeswold taking part in a Bullseye exercise that night. The weather was poor, with low cloud and wintry showers, and both aircraft flew into high ground while flying in cloud. A similar fate befell Sgt W A Catron (X3941) from No 27 OTU at Church Broughton while also taking part in a Bullseye exercise.

Crashes were a frequent feature of OTU flying, although many of them were not fatal. Some were caused by mishandling, pilot error or inaccurate navigation, while others reflected the poor state of health of the engines in OTU aircraft. In the first half of March 1943, aircraft losses at Nos 21, 22 and 23 OTUs included five non-fatal hull losses. On 1 March Plt Off E Harrison (HE484) from No 23 OTU suffered an engine failure at night, so the crew abandoned the aircraft, and Sgt P L Logan (HF674) from No 22 OTU experienced a double engine failure and force-landed at Gaydon. Four days later, Sgt B Job (R1601) from No 21 OTU crashed on landing at Honiley, and on 13 March Sgt C W Jackson (BK346) crashed on overshoot at Stratford. Finally, on 15 March, Sgt J S MacLeod (DF567) from No 22 OTU stalled and crashed at Gaydon.

These accidents were interspersed with more serious fatal crashes. Sgt R V Moss (BK433) and his crew from No 12 OTU were killed on 5 March when they stalled and spun in at Chipping Warden, and Sgt J H Lawson (X9792) and his crew from No 11 OTU lost their lives when they stalled while attempting to go around at Westcott ten days later.

The 'low risk' 'nickelling' sorties flown at the end of the course could also prove disastrous. On the night of 11/12 June, while the main bomber force attacked targets in the Ruhr, 23 pupil crews from the OTUs were tasked with carrying out 'nickelling' operations over northern France. One of these was Flt Sgt T G Dellar's BK559, which became lost over France and ran out of fuel near

The wreckage of Wellington IC DV653 of No 22 OTU, which crashed into the watch office at Stratford during night flying on 25 September 1942. Miraculously, Sgt J W Dunford and his crew were unhurt, except for the rear gunner, Sgt M R Foran, who was killed (*Philip Jarrett*)

Paris. Although three of the crew abandoned the aircraft, the pilot and navigator remained with it and were killed when it crashed. On the night of 22/23 June Sgt J Hennessey's HE527 of No 30 OTU was hit by flak over Cherbourg. Three crew bailed out and were captured and three were killed.

At the end of June 1943, the Air Order of Battle of the Wellington OTUs within Bomber Command was as follows;

No 91 Group

Harwell/Grove	No 15 OTU (EO, FH, KK)
Lossiemouth/Elgin	No 20 OTU (AI, HJ, JM, MK, XL, YR, ZT)
Moreton-in-Marsh/Enstone	No 21 OTU (ED, SJ, UH)
Wellesbourne Mountford/Stratford	No 22 OTU (DD, LT, OX, XN)
Pershore/Defford	No 23 OTU (BY, FZ, WE)

No 92 Group

Westcott/Oakley	No 11 OTU (KH, KJ, LG, OP, TX)
Chipping Warden/Edgehill	No 12 OTU (FQ, JP, ML)
Cottesmore/Saltby	No 14 OTU (AM, GL, VB)
Upper Heyford/Barford St John	No 16 OTU (GA, JS, XG)
Silverstone/Turweston	No 17 OTU (AY, JG, WJ)
Wing/Oakley	No 26 OTU (EU, PB, WG)
Bruntingthorpe/Bitteswell	No 29 OTU (TF)

No 93 Group

Finningley/Worksop	No 18 (Polish) OTU (EN, VQ, XW)
Lichfield/Church Broughton	No 27 OTU (BB, UJ, YC, YL)
Wymeswold/Castle Donington	No 28 OTU (LB, QN, WY)
Hixon/Seighford	No 30 OTU (BT, KD, TN)
Ossington/Bircotes	No 82 OTU (9C, BZ, KA, TD)

As the Wellington gave way to four-engined 'heavies' in the frontline, its importance in the operational training role increased. When Wellington squadrons converted to other types, more aircraft were released for training use. The Wellington's docile handling characteristics and rugged construction made it an ideal type in which crews could learn their trade. The emphasis at the OTUs altered slightly during 1943 in that they no longer acted as a conversion unit, as they had when so many bomber squadrons operated the Wellington. Instead, OTUs became the lead-in for the Heavy Conversion Unit course that introduced crews to their operational type.

But operational missions continued to be part of the final phase of the OTU syllabus. Usually, these were 'nickelling' sorties, but on occasions OTU crews were involved in mine laying sorties too. For rookie crews, the first taste of operations could be somewhat bewildering, and mistakes were made. Sgt J Kirkup (BK444), a pupil on No 29 OTU, took off from Bruntingthorpe at 2225 hrs on 29/30 July 1943 for a 'nickelling' sortie to Rennes. He later reported;

'We had a little trouble locating our pin-point on the coast owing to my mistaking the Cherbourg peninsula for Guernsey, and I altered course on my own initiative, informing the navigator I was doing so. I flew southwest for about ten minutes before realising my mistake, and then we had to re-start our air plot and carry on as before. We crossed the coast at the allotted position, but no member of the crew saw the photoflash explode. Apart from these two difficulties, the trip was very interesting and most instructive. The visibility was extremely good over the target area, as it was over the whole route apart from the Channel itself. We all thoroughly enjoyed the trip – even the navigator, who carried on philosophically, despite my attempt to ruin his working.'

Unfortunately, Gp Capt W C Sheen, Senior Air Staff Officer No 92 Group, did not find this report amusing, and wrote, 'I will take this matter up with Bruntingthorpe', further reporting that a letter was to be placed on Kirkup's file about his lack of crew cooperation.

After augmenting the main bombing force in mid-1942, the OTUs were not called for main force operations during the winter of 1942–43 or through the following summer. Apart from end-of-course 'nickelling' and 'gardening' sorties, the first time that OTU crews were used on operations in 1943 was on the night of 30/31 August, when 33 aircraft, including five from No 21 OTU, were tasked to bomb an ammunition depot in the Forêt d'Eperlecques near St Omer. Another 30 Wellingtons from the OTUs attacked similar depots in northern France on the following three nights. The purpose of these raids was to afford OTU crews the opportunity to practise bombing on Pathfinder target markers. Sgt T A Wilder (BJ967) of No 29 OTU took off from Bruntingthorpe on 30 August loaded with six 500-lb GP bombs, and his post-mission report gives a vivid picture of the sortie's abrupt ending;

'The target was very clearly defined by PFF Markers. Went in and bombed on a heading of 160°M and immediately turned and set course for Le Touquet. Pinpointed French coast at Le Touquet and ran over a thinnish layer of stratus cloud which obscured sea and English coast. On ETA Beachy Head, altered course Abingdon, height about 6000 ft. A few minutes after this the starboard engine caught fire. Throttled back for a moment or two and tried opening up again gently – engine still on fire. Took appropriate action and continued flying on one engine. Height now about 4500 ft, losing height fairly rapidly.

'Could now see searchlights and other small lights below me, immediately started looking for aerodrome, none to be seen. Called "Darky" [Mayday] four times – no response. Rear gunner reported it was his opinion that we were still over the sea. Endeavoured to confirm this by switching on landing light vertically downwards. Nothing seen at first but when at about 800 ft on altimeter could just make out wave tops. Crew had previously been ordered to crash-landing stations and were now ordered to prepare for ditching. Flotation bags were inflated, SOS sent out and all preparations made. Headed into wind and when W/Op called

Groundcrew from No 21 OTU relax at Moreton-in-Marsh prior to loading the 10-lb smoke bombs lying on the grass behind them. In the distance are four visiting USAAF B-17s (*Wellington Aviation*)

50-50, lowered 30° of flap. This almost immediately came off again and aircraft hit the water at 100–110 mph, starboard wing appearing to hit the water and cause a violent swerve to the right. I was plunged under water and struck my head on something. Released my harness and eventually came to the surface 15 to 20 yards away from machine, which appeared to have broken up. The dinghy was just inflating and I managed to reach it after a struggle.

'While hanging on to the side of the dinghy, trying to recover, I noticed one of the flotation bags drifting away from the machine, which was sinking rapidly. I then heard one shout, to which I replied by shouting loudly and blowing my whistle. I was not yet in the dinghy and no further shouts were heard. I eventually managed to board the dinghy in a state of exhaustion. As soon as I could I paddled round amongst the bits of wreckage, calling and blowing the whistle but to no avail. I then resigned myself to wait for dawn, the dinghy drifting westward meanwhile. About 20 minutes after ditching I noticed aircraft circling the scene of the crash and dropping flares but was too weak and upset to signal to them. Searchlights were also sweeping the sea from the cliffs. The dinghy drifted westward until at dawn I was 15 to 20 miles off Newhaven. After firing three Very cartridges with no results, at about 1030 hrs two Spitfires and a Walrus were seen coming in my direction. I immediately fired off another cartridge and was seen. The Walrus came down and picked me up and taxied back to Newhaven.'

Even in the summer months, non-operational sorties also continued to take their toll. Two examples of fatal accidents in August and September are typical of the losses suffered by OTU pupils. On the night of 18/19 August Flt Sgt A M Lovelle-Draper (BJ587) from No 12 OTU got airborne from Chipping Warden for a Bullseye exercise, which involved routing northwestwards out over western Scotland, thence to Northern Ireland and back to base. However, the aircraft failed to return from the sortie. The bodies of some of the crew were later washed up in the Solway Firth. Sgt R G Lees (LN532) from No 16 OTU was tasked with a Bullseye exercise on 28/29 September. This time the routing was southwards to Poole, before turning north to carry out a simulated bombing pass at the infra-red bombing range at Conwy. Four hours after it had taken off, the aircraft descended through the 800-ft cloud base and flew into the ground near Towcester.

The last main force bomber operation by a Bomber Command Wellington was flown by No 300 (Polish) Sqn in October 1943. Although this sortie marked the final demise of the Wellington as an operational type in Bomber Command, it coincided with the zenith of the Wellington as an OTU training machine. Two more Wellington OTUs were formed in the autumn of 1943, No 83 OTU at Childs Ercall in August and, the following month, No 84 OTU at Desborough. The oldest of the Wellington OTUs, No 15 OTU disbanded at Harwell in March 1944, with its place being taken by No 24 OTU at Honeybourne – it finally converted from the Whitley to the Wellington in April.

In June 1944, the strength of the Wellington OTUs within Bomber Command reached its peak with the formation of No 85 OTU at Husbands Bosworth and No 86 OTU at Gamston, as well as the conversion in the same month of No 10 OTU from the Whitley. At the end of June there were 22 bomber OTUs equipped with the Wellington;

No 91 Group

Abingdon/Stanton Harcourt	No 10 OTU (JL, RK, UY, ZG)
Kinloss/Forres	No 19 OTU (UO, XF, ZV)
Lossiemouth/Milltown	No 20 OTU (AI, HJ, JM, MK, XL, YR, ZT)
Moreton in Marsh/Enstone	No 21 OTU (ED, SJ, UH)
Wellesbourne Mountford/Gaydon	No 22 OTU (DD, LT, OX, XN)
Honeybourne/Long Marston	No 24 OTU (FB, TY, UF)

No 92 Group

Westcott/Oakley	No 11 OTU (KH, KJ, LG, OP, TX)
Chipping Warden/Edge Hill	No 12 OTU (FQ, JP, ML)
Market Harborough	No 14 OTU (AM, GL, VB)
Upper Heyford/Barford St John	No 16 OTU (GA, JS, XG)
Silverstone/Turweston	No 17 OTU (AY, JG, WJ)
Wing/Oakley	No 26 OTU (EU, PB, WG)
Bruntingthorpe/Bitteswell	No 29 OTU (TF)
Desborough/Harrington	No 84 OTU (CO, CZ, IF)
Husbands Bosworth	No 85 OTU (9P, 2X)
Gamston	No 86 OTU (Y7)

No 93 Group

Finningley/Worksop	No 18 (Polish) OTU (EN, VQ, XW)
Lichfield/Church Broughton	No 27 OTU (BB, UJ, YC, YL)
Wymeswold/Castle Donnington	No 28 OTU (LB, QN, WY)
Hixon/Seighford	No 30 OTU (BT, KD, TN)
Ossington/Bircotes	No 82 OTU (9C, BZ, KA, TD)
Peplow	No 83 OTU (FI, GS, MZ)

The Wellington continued to be used for the training of crews until war's end, as the bomber offensive reached its climax. But like the frontline units that they supported, the OTUs quickly disappeared after victory had been achieved. Most were disbanded in June and July 1945, although Wellington T 10s continued to serve with Training Command units into the early 1950s.

Groundcrew ready 13 Wellington IIIs (all with their bomb-bay doors open) from No 30 OTU at Hixon on 11 September 1943. The image is perhaps typical of the daily scene at many of the Wellington OTU airfields (*Graham Pitchfork*)

APPENDICES

COLOUR PLATES

1

Wellington I L4288/KA-ZA of No 9 Sqn, Honington, 1939
This aircraft is painted in standard day bomber Pattern 'A' markings, which were applied to aircraft with even numbered serials. The roundels have been overpainted from 'Type A' to the toned down 'Type B' version. The No 9 Sqn crest (a bat in flight) has been painted beneath the cockpit. This aircraft was destroyed in a mid-air collision with L4320 on 30 October 1939 while practising a formation cross-over manoeuvre. Sqn Ldr L S Lamb and his crew, as well as the crew of L4320, were killed.

2

Wellington I L4257/LY-P of No 149 Sqn, Mildenhall, 1939
The aircraft is painted in standard day bomber Pattern 'B' markings, as applied to aircraft with odd numbered serials. The roundels have also been overpainted from 'Type A' to the toned down 'Type B'. It flew into the sea off Happisburgh during firing practice on 29 August 1939 and Sgt O T V Pitt and his crew were killed.

3

Wellington I L4367 of No 75 Sqn, Honington, 1939
The aircraft is in standard day bomber camouflage, overpainted with temporary markings for the annual Home Defence Air Exercises that were held in August 1939. The white crosses indicate L4367 is part of the 'friendly' Westland forces. This aircraft was transferred to No 11 OTU at Bassingbourn on its formation in 1940.

4

Wellington I NZ305 of the 'New Zealand Squadron', Marham, 1939
This aircraft was the last of the Wellingtons taken on charge by the New Zealand government pre-war. It was finished in the standard RAF colour scheme Pattern 'A', with RAF markings. After the declaration of war, the aircraft reverted to its Air Ministry serial number L4360 and was transferred to No 15 OTU on its formation in 1940. The bomber subsequently moved to No 20 OTU and was damaged beyond repair on 29 June 1941 when Plt Off G A Watt overshot the runway while landing at Lossiemouth, causing the undercarriage to collapse.

5

Wellington IA P9299/BK-U of No 115 Sqn, Marham, 1939
Painted in the standard day bomber markings Pattern 'B', P9299 was issued to No 115 Sqn in April 1940. It was then passed on to No 218 Sqn in December 1940 and, the following year, to No 1429 Flight (Czech OTU) at East Wretham. P9299 was destroyed on 6 April 1942 when it flew into a hillside near Llanymawddwy on the River Dovey, killing Sgt A Keda and his all-Czech crew.

6

Wellington IA N2871/WS-B of No 9 Sqn, Honington, December 1939
This aircraft was flown by Flg Off W J Macrae during the ill-fated raid on Wilhelmshaven on 18 December 1939. Macrae was in the section led by Sqn Ldr A J Guthrie, which was on Wg Cdr Kellett's port side. The whole section was savaged by fighters and four of the six aircraft, including Guthrie's, were shot down. Macrae's Wellington was badly damaged and he made a forced landing at North Coates.

7

Wellington IA N2912/LG-G of No 215 Sqn, Bassingbourn, 1940
This aircraft was passed on to No 11 OTU when No 215 Sqn merged into the training unit in April 1940. It carries the more visible national markings introduced in 1940. The aircraft remained with the OTU until it was shot down by a night intruder on 24 Apr 1941 while on night circuit training at Bassingbourn. N2912 crashed onto the airfield and hit Wellington R1404 crewed by Sgt F N Alstrom, which was parked in one of the dispersals. The pilot of N2912, Sgt P N Nicholls, survived, but the two remaining crew were killed.

8

Wellington IA N2985/AA-M of No 75 Sqn, Harwell, 1940
This aircraft carries the high visibility markings introduced in 1940 after operational experience highlighted the difficulty of identifying aircraft with toned-down markings. The size and placement of the tail flash was not standardized until later in the year, and varied from unit to unit. At Harwell, No 75 Sqn carried out armament and operational training until it merged with No 148 Sqn to form No 15 OTU. N2985 has been modified to give greater clearance between the front turret and the fuselage immediately behind it – a modification more associated with the Mk IC.

9

Wellington IA P9273/OJ-N of No 149 Sqn, Mildenhall, 1940
This aircraft is finished in the night camouflage that was introduced in the second half of 1940. The black RDM2 paint was applied to the aircraft's sides up to a scalloped border with the dark green/dark earth disruptive pattern on the uppersurfaces. The fin, also painted black, featured a small tail flash on its leading edge. P9273 failed to return from a mission to Kiel on 10 October 1940, Flg Off R G Furness and his crew being killed.

10

Wellington IC R3297/AA-S of No 75 (NZ) Sqn, Feltwell, September 1940
Unofficial 'nose art' started to appear on operational aircraft in 1940 – in this case, the cartoon is based on Capt Bruce Bairnsfather's 'Old Bill' cartoon character. The size and placement of the tail flash had been standardised by the latter half of 1940 to the rectangle ahead of the rudder. R3297 was flown by Plt Off D J Harkness on operations with this unit until the bomber was transferred to No 57 Sqn in 1941.

11

Wellington IC R1410/KX-M of No 311 (Czech) Sqn, East Wretham, 1941
R1410's white circle in its roundel has been crudely painted black in order to make the aircraft less visible to nightfighters. This measure failed to prevent the aircraft from being damaged during a raid on Hanover on 15 May 1941. Although the port engine caught fire, Flt Lt J Snajdr was able to fly the aircraft home on one engine and belly

land near Manningtree. The bomber was repaired and transferred to No 12 OTU at Benson, where it retained No 311 Sqn codes. On 26 June 1942, during the period when OTU crews were being used to augment frontline squadrons, it was shot down northwest of Terschelling and Sgt J T Shapcott and his crew were killed.

12
Wellington IC N2856/LN-V of No 99 Sqn, Waterbeach, 1941
After much debate and experimentation, the position for the fuselage-mounted 'beam guns' on the Wellington IC was eventually finalised in late 1940. The result was the distinctive triangular-shaped windows in the rear fuselage sides of some aircraft. The artwork on this aeroplane is the musical notation for the opening bars of Beethoven's Symphony No 5 in C minor, which also represents the Morse Code for the letter 'V'. N2856 was transferred to No 12 OTU at Benson and used for operational missions during May and June 1942.

13
Wellington IC W5690/GR-W of No 301 (Polish) Sqn, Hemswell, 1941
Four Polish squadrons flew Wellingtons in Bomber Command. The artwork on this aircraft depicts the Red Griffin badge of 41 *Eskadra Rozpoznawcza* (41 Reconnaissance Squadron) of 4 *Pułk Lotniczy* (4 Aviation Regiment) of the *Lotnictwo Wojska Polskiego* (Polish Army Aviation). The Griffin had been painted on the PZL.23 Karaś flown by the unit at the beginning of the war. After service with No 301 (Polish) Sqn, W5690 was transferred to No 103 Sqn, then to No 20 OTU and finally to No 15 OTU, where it crashed on 16 November 1943 during circuit flying at Hampstead Norris.

14
Wellington IC W5612/PM-G of No 103 Sqn, Elsham Wolds, 1941
Many RAF aircraft were paid for by groups or countries during World War 2, and W5612 was the second presentation aircraft from Sierra Leone. Note how the fuselage windows above the wing have been partially blanked off. The aircraft was newly delivered when it flew its first operational mission against Brest on 30/31 March 1941. On its return, the aircraft was orbiting Elsham Wold while a minor unserviceability was being resolved when it was attacked by a night intruder. W5612 crash-landed a mile from base, and the only casualty was Sqn Ldr K J Mellor, who was slightly injured.

15
Wellington IC R1697/NZ-S of No 304 (Polish) Sqn, Lindholme, April 1942
In late 1940, No 304 (Polish) Sqn became the third Polish Wellington unit to form in Bomber Command. Like all the Polish squadrons, a small Polish flag was painted beneath the cockpit. Note how the fuselage windows above the wing have been completely blanked off. The aircraft was written off in a forced landing at Lindholme on 25 April 1942, the bomber having been damaged (and pilot Sqn Ldr K Czetowicz wounded) by a Bf 110 nightfighter over Flensburg.

16
Wellington IC X3175/BH-L of No 300 (Polish) Sqn, Hemswell, 1941
Another of the Polish units in Bomber Command, No 300 (Polish) Sqn converted from Battles and flew its first mission in December

1940. The impressive tally of bomb symbols painted around the Polish flag indicate the good fortune of the crew who flew this machine. X3175 continued to enjoy good luck, surviving further operations after being transferred to No 150 Sqn in December 1941, before moving to No 21 OTU at Moreton-in-Marsh.

17
Wellington II W5461/EP-R of No 104 Sqn, Driffield, 1941
The distinctive shape of the Merlin engines made the Wellington II easily identifiable. The fuselage was similar to that of the Mk IC, including the positions of the beam gun mountings, which, like those in the Mk IC, varied. W5461 was shot down on 13 August 1941 during a raid on Berlin. Sqn Ldr H Budden and his crew abandoned the aircraft and were captured.

18
Wellington II W5567/SM-M of No 305 (Polish) Sqn, Lindholme, 1942
Unusually, the tally of missions for this aircraft were recorded on the fin, rather than beneath the cockpit. Aside from the Polish flag on the nose, this aircraft is also adorned with a temporary cartoon drawn in chalk depicting 'Popeye the Sailor' taking a swipe at Hitler's head, with the motto *WE ARE THE STRONGEST YA BIG LUMMOX!!* W5567 was downed by flak over Lübeck on 29 March 1942, Sgt F Wasinski and his crew surviving as PoWs.

19
Wellington II W5430/PH-R of No 12 Sqn, Binbrook, 1941
One of the few units to be exclusively equipped with Wellington IIs, No 12 Sqn also standardised the placement of nose art between the front turret and the lozenge-shaped window in the nose. On this aircraft, successful missions were marked by a beer glass under the depiction of Robin Hood and a night owl. W5430 was damaged beyond repair when it overshot the runway at Binbrook after returning from an aborted sortie to Köln on 30 July 1941 with a full bombload still on board. Sgt W G Cooper and his crew escaped unhurt.

20
Wellington III X3763/KW-E of No 425 Sqn RCAF, Dishforth, 1943
The Wellington III was identifiable by the carburettor intakes above and below the cowling of the Hercules engine, as well as the four-gun Nash & Thompson FN-20A tail turret. The fuselage windows above the wings were deleted and the triangular aft window housing the beam gun became standard on this variant. During 1942, unit codes began to be painted in red. X3763 was downed on 15 April 1943 near Mussy-sur-Seine, Plt Off A T Douchette RCAF and his crew being killed.

21
Wellington III X3662/KO-P of No 115 Sqn, Mildenhall, 1942
This Wellington is depicted in its last days of service with No 115 Sqn, having survived 36 operational missions with the unit. At that stage of the war, the average life of a frontline bomber was only 11 missions. Transferred to No 20 OTU at Lossiemouth, X3662 crashed into the sea off Dunvegan Head, on the northwest tip of the Isle of Skye, at about 0600 hrs on 8 October 1943 while carrying out a navigation exercise. Flt Sgt G F Smith RCAF and his crew were killed in the accident.

22
Wellington III Z1572/VR-Q of No 419 Sqn RCAF, Mildenhall, May 1942
Initially allocated to No 115 Sqn, then to No 75 (NZ) Sqn, Z1572 suffered damage during a raid on Dortmund on 14/15 April 1942. After repairs, it was passed on to No 419 Sqn and took part in the 'thousand-bomber raid' on Köln on 30/31 May, with Plt Off B N Jost RCAF at the controls. In October 1942 Z1572 was passed on to No 427 Sqn RCAF, and it later also served with No 16 OTU at Upper Heyford.

23
Wellington III BK347/BT-Z of No 30 OTU, Hixon, 1943
Initially flown as 'Z' by No 30 OTU, BK347 had become 'Q' by the time its crew became lost in deteriorating weather on a cross-country flight from Hixon on 21 April 1944. Unfortunately, they were 150 miles off course, and when pilot Flg Off E M Barrett tried to descend below cloud to fix a position, he flew into high ground at Whernside, near Ingleton in North Yorkshire. Barrett and four crewmen were killed, with only rear gunner Sgt J Marks surviving the crash.

24
Wellington IV Z1320/BH-K of No 300 (Polish) Sqn, Hemswell, 1942
The Wellington IV was distinguishable from the Mk III by the smaller nacelles and carburettor intakes of the Pratt & Witney Twin Wasp engines and two-gun tail turret. Z1320 initially served with No 458 Sqn RAAF, where it acquired the 'artwork' depicting the stars of the Southern Cross. Transferred to No 300 (Polish) Sqn in 1942, the bomber failed to return from a sortie to Bremen on 5 September 1942 after almost certainly being shot down into the sea by a nightfighter. Flg Off A Szpak and crew were killed.

25
Wellington X HZ376/BH-G of No 300 (Polish) Sqn, Hemswell, 1943
Outwardly similar to the Mk III, the main distinguishing feature of the Wellington X was the elongated carburettor intakes above the engine nacelles. This aircraft was downed by flak on the night of 24/25 June 1943 during the raid on Wuppertal. Pilot Flg Off W Turecki and the rear gunner survived to become PoWs, but the remaining three crewmen were killed.

26
Wellington X X3595/AA-K of No 18 (Polish) OTU, Finningley, 1942
This aircraft was originally built at Blackpool as a Wellington III, and it served briefly with No 75 (NZ) Sqn during March 1942. Subsequently sent to the Vickers factory at Weybridge, the bomber was fitted with Bristol Hercules VI engines to become the prototype Wellington X.

During this period, the bomber retained the markings of No 75 (NZ) Sqn, and X3595 is depicted here as it appeared upon arrival at No 18 (Polish) OTU in 1942. The aircraft also later served with Nos 15 and 22 OTUs.

27
Wellington X HZ279/HD-R of No 466 Sqn RAAF, Driffield, 1943
The artwork on this Wellington depicts the character 'Father William' from Younger's Brewery. Its adoption was a play on the name of the aircraft captain from March 1943, Flg Off R A L Young RAFVR. Completed operational missions are recorded by beer tankards. Note that the front turret has been sealed and the guns removed. The aircraft remained with No 466 Sqn RAAF until June 1943, when it was transferred to No 11 OTU. HZ279 was eventually struck off charge in 1948. Raymond Young was killed in action on 9 October 1943.

28
Wellington X NC427/TY-B of No 24 OTU, Honeybourne, 1944
By mid-1944 22 bomber OTUs were equipped with the Wellington. Based at Honeybourne and Long Marston, No 24 OTU was one of the last to receive the Wellington, having previously operated Whitleys. Note that guns are only fitted to the rear turret – gunnery pupils practised firing from the rear turret against a drogue that was towed behind the aircraft. Once the drogue had been streamed, gentle turns would make it snake through the air, creating a more challenging target.

29
Wellington IC P2521/MA-V of No 161 Sqn, Newmarket, 1942
P2521 was one of the first Wellingtons to be modified to become a Directional Wireless Installation (DWI) aircraft, and it were used by No 1 General Reconnaissance Unit of Coastal Command to clear magnetic sea mines. DWI Wellingtons had their turrets faired over and a large circular structure fitted that contained an electro-magnetic coil to trigger the mines. This aircraft was later returned to Bomber Command and, with the DWI equipment removed, it joined No 161 (Special Duties) Sqn when the unit was formed in 1942. The aircraft was used for radio interception work.

30
Wellington IC L7842/KX-T of the *Erprobungsstelle* Rechlin, Rechlin-Lärz, 1941
During a raid on Boulogne on 6 February 1941, Plt Off F Cigoš and his crew from No 311 (Czech) Sqn became lost and, thinking they were over England, landed at the nearest airfield before they ran out of fuel. Unfortunately, they had landed at Flers Saint-Paul, in Normandy. On realising their error, they attempted to take off again, but the aircraft became bogged down in soft ground and the crew were captured. The Luftwaffe salvaged the bomber and took it to the Test Centre at Rechlin for evaluation.

INDEX